MODERN DATA

FROM INGESTION TO PRODUCTION

MODERN DATA

STEPS TOWARD A FUTURE IN DATA ENGINEERING

KELVIN LIN

FIRST EDITION

Modern Data: From Ingestion to Production

ISBN: 9798348464271
Independently Published

Disclaimer: This book is intended for educational and informational purposes only. While every effort has been made to ensure accuracy, the author and publisher assume no responsibility for errors, omissions, or damages resulting from the use of the information contained herein. Examples, screenshots, and scenarios are provided for illustration and educational commentary. Logos, trademarks, and website images remain the property of their respective owners and are used here under fair use principles for descriptive and educational purposes. No endorsement by, or affiliation with, any company or organization is implied.

Cover Design: Madison Mercado
Printed in the United States of America
First Edition, 2026

To my family,
for giving me the opportunity
to pursue knowledge.

CONTENTS

Introduction

Why Data Engineering?

"The purpose of computing is insight, not numbers."

– Richard Hamming [1]

In the modern world, nearly every interaction generates data. When you stream music, order food through an app, or even tap your credit card at the store, those small actions produce digital traces. Yet raw data on its own does not drive decisions or build products. The systems that collect, organize, and transform it into something useful are designed by data engineers. They are the professionals who create the pipelines and platforms that turn chaotic information into business value.

Data engineering is no longer a niche technical role. It's one of the fastest growing careers in technology and business. While the U.S. Bureau of Labor Statistics (BLS) doesn't publish a separate category for data engineers, related roles provide a strong indicator of growth. For example, employment of data scientists is projected to grow 34 percent from 2024 to 2034, much faster than the average for all occupations. Database administrators and architects are expected to grow at about 4 percent, and software developers at about 15–16 percent over the same period [2], [3]. Industry reports also highlight that demand for data engineers is expanding rapidly, with many organizations creating new roles as they recognize the need for clean, reliable, and well-structured data to compete in a digital economy.

The career outlook is equally attractive when it comes to compensation. The average salary for data engineers in the United States is about 130,000 dollars per year, with entry-level engineers starting around 100,000 dollars and senior engineers earning more than 150,000 dollars, according to Glassdoor data [4]. In technology hubs such as the San Francisco Bay Area, salaries can rise above 200,000 dollars, especially at major companies like Google, Meta, and Dropbox. This level of compensation reflects the critical role data engineers play in modern organizations, where a broken pipeline can mean millions in lost revenue or missed insights.

What sets data engineering apart is its centrality. Without data engineers, data science models cannot be trained, dashboards cannot be built, and executives cannot make informed decisions. The entire ecosystem of analytics, artificial intelligence (AI), and digital transformation depends on the reliability of the infrastructure that data engineers design. They are often described as the backbone of successful organizations because they enable everyone else to succeed with data.

For those considering a career path, data engineering offers more than stability and salary. It provides the opportunity to work at the intersection of technology, strategy, and innovation. Whether in finance, healthcare, e-commerce, or government, every sector is leaning on data engineering to power its future. That makes this a field worth mastering.

In this book, I'll walk you through the world of data engineering, from its foundational concepts to real-world applications. We'll explore how raw data is extracted, transformed, and loaded into systems where it can deliver value. Along the way, I'll break down the modern data stack, highlight the tools that power today's most data-driven companies, and walk through the principles that separate good pipelines from great ones. Whether you're just starting out or looking to deepen your expertise, this book aims to make the complex systems behind data engineering both accessible and actionable.

Chapter 1
History of Data Engineering

"The best way to predict the future is to invent it."

– Alan Kay [5]

Historic Data Engineering

Every company today claims it wants to "become more data-driven." But the truth is, people have been data-driven for thousands of years.

We observed, measured, remembered, and acted on information out of necessity. Spotting animal tracks, tracking seasons, and learning from patterns in nature weren't optional. Rather, it was necessary for survival. In many ways, data engineering is just a modern extension of those ancient instincts, only now the datasets are bigger, and the stakes are measured in dollars instead of dinner.

For most of human history, data was physical: etched on clay tablets, scribbled in ledgers, stored in human memory. Ancient Egyptians recorded grain inventories and cultivable land [6]. Babylonians tracked celestial movements to predict seasons [7]. The Ancient Greeks kept detailed recorded voting outcomes from early democratic assemblies [8]. Early data "engineering" was done with pen and parchment and required discipline, logic, and long hours. These systems are archaic to us, sure, but they had structure: columns, rows, dates, categories. The ideas behind data schemas existed long before relational databases did.

While the term "data engineering" didn't exist until much later, the functions associated with it like moving data between systems, defining data structures, and ensuring consistency were already present in the era of hierarchical and network databases in the mid 20th century.

These early systems, like IBM's Information Management System (IMS) conceptualized in the 1960s, which stored data in a tree-like structure, and the CODASYL network model, which used a more flexible graph of predefined relationships, required engineers to manually define relationships, optimize access paths, and write complex low-level procedural code to retrieve data [9], [10]. Working with these databases demanded deep technical knowledge of the schema and system architecture, which meant that in practice, data access was limited to a small group of trained specialists.

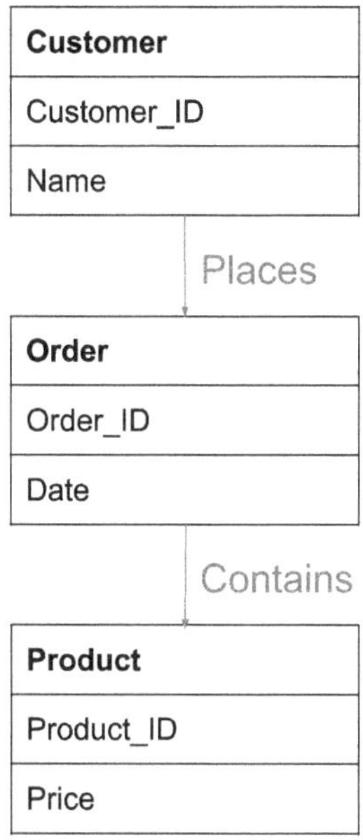

Figure 1: Simple CODAYSL Model

The shift from this rigid, expert-only approach to the more accessible and modular form of data engineering we recognize today didn't truly begin until the invention of the relational database by Edgar F. Codd, a British computer scientist at IBM, in the 1970s [11].

In his revolutionary paper, *A Relational Model of Data for Large Shared Data Banks*, Codd proposed a new model that directly addressed the limitations of the hierarchical and network databases that came before it. Specifically, he wrote:

"The relational view (or model) of data ... appears to be superior in several respects to the graph or network model ... It provides a means of describing data with its natural structure only—that is, without superimposing any additional structure for machine representation purposes [12]."

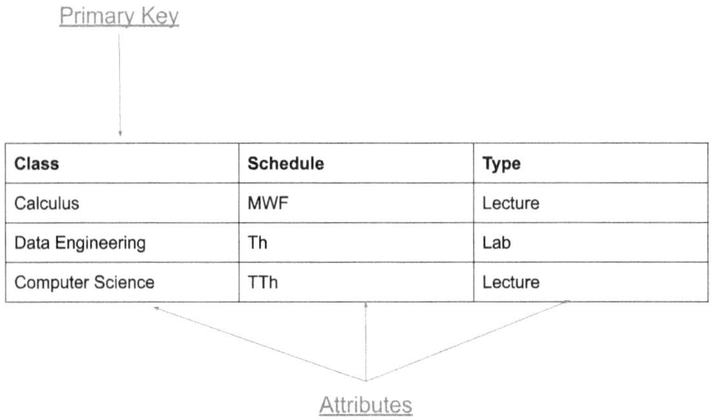

Figure 2: The Simple Relational Model

What Codd highlighted here was simple but profound. He argued that data should be modeled based on its real-world meaning, not the internal logic of how machines store or retrieve it. In doing so, he separated the logical structure of data (the relationship it represents) from its physical storage (how it's actually saved on disk).

This principle changed everything. It meant that engineers no longer had to manually define traversal paths, worry about pointer chains, or embed access logic directly into their application code. Instead, they could describe what data they wanted, and let the database engine figure out how to get it.

As a continuation of Codd's work, a team of IBM researchers began working on an experimental relational database system called System R in 1974 [13], [14]. The project was a success. Not only did it prove that relational databases could achieve competitive performance, it also laid the groundwork for what would eventually become the Structured Query Language or SQL, now the industry standard for interacting with relational data today.

Originally dubbed the Structured English Querying Language or SEQUEL, the researchers designed a language that allowed users to interact with data in a human-friendly way [15]. By using phrases like SELECT, WHERE, JOIN, etc. which resembled plain English, they aimed to make querying accessible to non-technical users [16]. This eliminated the need for writing complex procedural code and allowed people to simply describe the data they wanted, rather than detailing how to retrieve it.

Due to a trademark discrepancy with a UK-based aerospace company, IBM dropped the vowels from SEQUEL and renamed the language SQL to avoid legal complications [15]. Despite the change in spelling, many still continue to pronounce it as "sequel."

The success of System R and SQL didn't stay confined to IBM's labs. By the early 1980s, companies like Oracle, Ingres, and IBM itself had begun commercializing relational databases. SQL became the de facto standard, adopted not just by technologists but by entire organizations. It became the foundation for countless enterprise systems, from payroll to inventory management and helped businesses turn operational data into strategic insight.

This was the era when the data engineer role started to take shape. While it wasn't always called that, professionals were now tasked with designing schemas, building ETL pipelines, maintaining data integrity, and making data accessible across departments.

As organizations began collecting more data than ever before, a new challenge emerged: how do you store and analyze massive volumes of historical data across different systems, departments, and use cases? Traditional relational databases were optimized for transactions, that being things like updating a record, retrieving a customer profile, or processing an order. But they weren't designed to support large-scale analytics over time.

Modern Data Engineering

The solution came in the concept of data warehousing, formalized in the 1990s by computer scientist Bill Inmon, who is widely regarded as the father of the data warehouse. According to Inmon, a data warehouse is not a specific technology but an architectural approach to managing data to support analysis and decision-making. As he defines it in *Building the Data Warehouse*, "A data warehouse is a subject-oriented, integrated, nonvolatile, and time-variant collection of data in support of management's decisions."

Inmon emphasized that this distinction between architecture and technology is essential to understand. As he elegantly puts it: "There is the architecture, then there is the underlying technology, and they are two very different things. Unquestionably, there is a relationship between data warehousing and database technology, but they are most certainly not the same. Data warehousing requires the support of many different kinds of technology [17]."

Inmon was a proponent of a top-down approach to data warehousing, where an enterprise-wide data model is designed first, and individual data marts are created afterward to serve specific business needs. Instead of focusing on just one department at a time, the company would take a big-picture view and design the structure of the warehouse to serve the entire organization. Once that foundation is in place, smaller pieces of the system (data marts) can be built to serve the needs of individual teams like sales, marketing, or customer service.

While a good idea in theory, in practice it faced many limitations. For example, when companies attempted to implement this, they often ran into the problem of long development timelines. Because the data warehouse had to be fully designed and built to serve

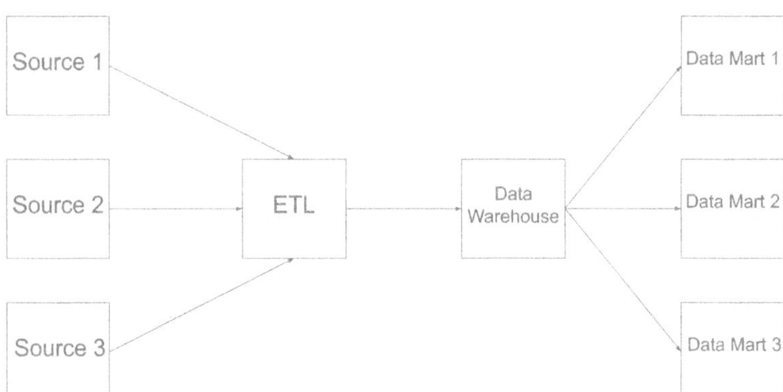

Figure 3: Inmon's Top-down Approach

the entire organization before any one team could use it, projects could take months or even years before delivering any real business value.

In addition to the delays, the initial cost of building such a large, centralized system was substantial. It required significant investment in infrastructure, tools, and specialized personnel. The approach also lacked flexibility. Business needs would often shift during development, but the rigid structure made it difficult to adapt quickly. Teams were frequently left waiting for updates or changes to be modeled and approved across the entire system before they could move forward [18].

These challenges left many organizations searching for a more practical and responsive alternative, something that could show results sooner and adjust as the business evolved.

Inmon's colleague Ralph Kimball proposed a different strategy, one that addressed many of the limitations found in the top-down model [19]. Instead of starting with a centralized data warehouse, Kimball suggested building individual data marts first. Each data mart would focus on a specific business area, such as sales, marketing, or inventory. These marts could then be connected using shared dimensions and rolled up into a broader data warehouse over time [20].

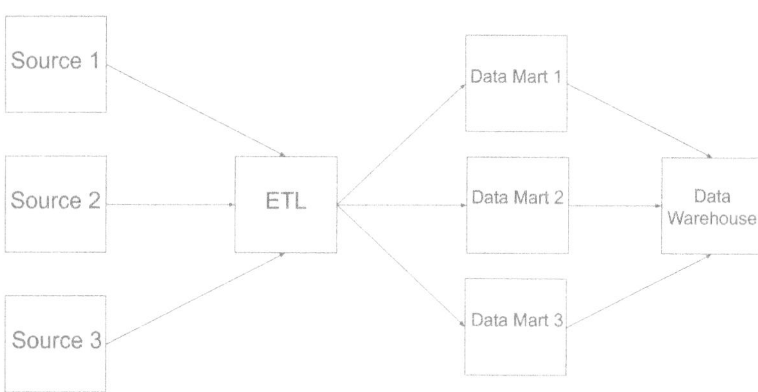

Figure 4: Kimball's Bottom-up Approach

This approach allowed for a much more agile way of building data infrastructure. Making changes no longer required reworking the entire system. Instead, teams could update or expand just the relevant data mart. The initial setup was also faster, making it easier for organizations to deliver value to the business early in the process, rather than waiting months or years for a fully centralized warehouse to be completed [21].

As data volumes continued to grow in the 2000s, traditional relational data warehouses began to show their limitations. Web-scale companies were now dealing with data that arrived continuously, in massive quantities, and in a variety of formats. This included user activity logs, clickstream data, product images, and free-form text which was far more complex than the clean, structured tables that warehouses were built to handle. These systems were expensive to scale, slow to adapt, and poorly suited for real-time or semi-structured data.

In response, engineers began turning to distributed computing systems, which distribute work across multiple machines to handle large workloads. Instead of relying on a single powerful server, these systems break a large task into smaller parts and run them in parallel on a cluster of computers. This is what gives the approach its name. It distributes both data and processing across a system.

This made it possible to store and analyze far larger datasets than traditional systems could handle. However, it also introduced new challenges. Engineers now had to figure out how to split the work effectively, manage coordination between machines, and design systems that were fault-tolerant (handle failures without losing progress or data). Despite the complexity, this shift enabled a level of scalability and speed that centralized warehouses simply could not achieve.

One of the most influential breakthroughs came from Google in 2004 with the introduction of the MapReduce abstraction. In the widely influential paper, *MapReduce: Simplified Data Processing on Large Clusters*, Google engineers Jeffrey Dean and Sanjay Ghemawat outlined a programming model that made it possible to process vast amounts of data in parallel across distributed systems [22].

The key idea was to split work into two simple operations: map, which applies a function to each record in a dataset and produces intermediate key-value pairs, and reduce, which aggregates or summarizes those pairs by key. For example, mapping could count the occurrence of each word in a document, while reducing would sum those counts across all documents. This approach abstracted away many of the complexities of distributed computing, allowing engineers to focus on writing simple "map" and "reduce" functions while the underlying system handled fault tolerance, data distribution, and execution.

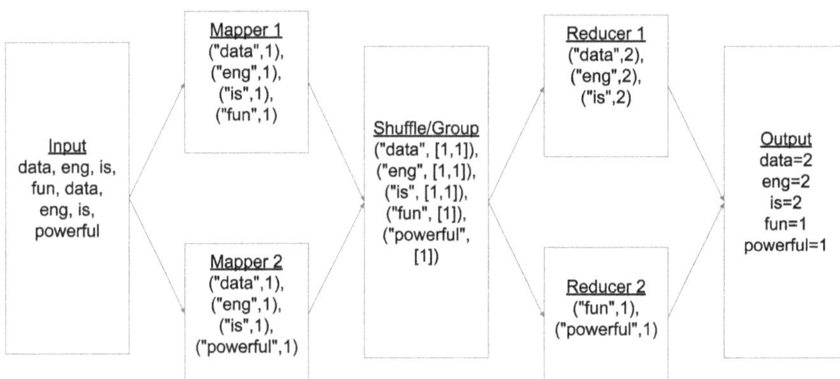

Figure 5: Simple MapReduce Example

The authors described a key challenge of the time: although the computations themselves were often conceptually simple, they became difficult to scale. As they put it, "The issues of how to parallelize the computation, distribute the data, and handle failures conspire to obscure the original simple computation with large amounts of complex code." MapReduce offered a way to simplify this, allowing developers to express their logic cleanly while the system took care of the difficult distributed systems engineering behind the scenes.

Inspired by the MapReduce paper, engineer Doug Cutting, along with Mike Cafarella, began building an open-source implementation. When the system outgrew its original purpose, they spun it out into a new Apache project, which Cutting named Hadoop, after his son's toy elephant [23].

With support from Yahoo!, Hadoop rapidly matured. As Cutting later reflected on his website, "After one year, Hadoop was used daily by many research groups within Yahoo!. After two years it generated Yahoo!'s web search index, achieving web-scale. Now, after three years, Hadoop holds the big-data sort record and the project has become a de-facto industry standard for big-data computing, used by scores of companies [24]."

The success of Hadoop was driven by Google's ideas and the engineering talent at Yahoo!. Their work made it possible for organizations outside of Big Tech to process data at scale using affordable, distributed infrastructure.

Despite its massive impact, Hadoop came with real challenges. It was powerful, but complex. Running a Hadoop cluster required deep technical expertise and significant operational overhead. Jobs were written in Java, making it inaccessible for analysts and business users. It was also fundamentally built for batch processing, which made it less suited for real-time analytics. As data grew faster and more diverse, and as companies sought more agile, cloud-friendly solutions, new tools began to emerge that prioritized simplicity, speed, and accessibility [25].

One of the most significant developments during this period was the emergence of Apache Spark. Initially developed at UC Berkeley's AMPLab in 2009, deployed in production by 2010, and later donated to the Apache Software Foundation in 2013, Spark was created to overcome many of the limitations of Hadoop and MapReduce.

Unlike previous systems, which required writing intermediate results to disk between steps, Spark supported running multiple operations over the same dataset in memory. This made it significantly more efficient for many workloads, especially those involving iterative processing like machine learning or data exploration. Spark introduced a flexible programming model through a concept called resilient distributed datasets (RDDs), which allowed for fault-tolerant, parallel computation.

Perhaps even more importantly, Spark offered unified APIs in accessible languages like Python and Scala, expanding its usability beyond Java developers. As of today, Spark supports Python, SQL, Scala, Java, and R, making it one of the most versatile platforms in the data engineering ecosystem.

Spark could handle batch, streaming, and interactive big data workloads, making it far more adaptable than MapReduce. It quickly became a popular choice for building ETL pipelines, powering streaming machine learning workflows, and scaling analytics efforts. While Spark retained compatibility with the Hadoop Distributed File System (HDFS), its emphasis on speed, flexibility, and developer productivity marked a major shift in how modern data systems were built [26].

Among the earliest breakthroughs in cloud-native analytics was Google BigQuery, launched in 2011. Based on Google's Dremel technology, BigQuery introduced a fully managed, serverless approach to querying massive datasets with SQL [27]. Around the same time, Amazon Redshift, launched in 2012, brought data warehousing to the Amazon Web Services ecosystem, allowing teams to migrate their analytical workloads into the cloud [28].

A few years later, Snowflake redefined expectations with a platform designed from the ground up for cloud computing. By separating storage from compute, Snowflake made it possible to scale workloads up or down instantly and support multiple users or teams without performance bottlenecks.

As these cloud data warehouses gained adoption, they were often paired with modern business intelligence platforms like Tableau, Microsoft Power BI, and Google Looker. These tools gave analysts and stakeholders the ability to explore data visually, build dashboards, and generate reports directly from the warehouse. This convergence of scalable storage, familiar query languages, and intuitive visualization marked the beginning of the modern analytics era.

And that brings us to where we are today. Data engineering is no longer just about moving data from one place to another. It's about designing systems that are scalable, reliable, and accessible across entire organizations. Engineers are expected to work across cloud platforms, orchestrate ETL/ELT workflows, maintain data quality, and empower analysts and stakeholders through well-modeled, accessible datasets.

The history of data engineering is the story of how we've learned to tame complexity at ever greater scales. What began as marks on clay tablets and ink in ledgers has evolved into massively parallel systems, real-time pipelines, and cloud-native platforms that power decisions across every modern industry. Each era, from relational databases to Hadoop to Spark and the modern data stack, emerged to solve the limitations of the last.

Today, data engineers sit at the center of this evolution. They build enterprise-grade systems that move and transform data, while also ensuring its reliability, accessibility, and trustworthiness across the organization. They are connectors between raw numbers and real-world insight.

Understanding how we got here provides context and direction for the future of our profession. The challenges we face today, whether that be scaling machine learning systems or maintaining data quality in real time, echo the same themes: how to handle more data, faster, with fewer errors, and greater impact.

Chapter 2

Defining the Data Engineer

"I'm not a great programmer; I'm just a good programmer with great habits"

– Kent Beck [29]

What isn't a Data Engineer?

In order to understand what exactly a data engineer is, it's essential to understand what a data engineer is NOT.

A data engineer is not a software engineer. Software engineers write code to build applications, services, and systems that end users interact with. Their focus is on performance, scalability, and maintainability in the context of building products. While data engineers also write production-quality code, their focus is on building and maintaining systems that move, transform, and organize data so that it's accurate and available when needed.

A data engineer is not a data analyst. Data analysts are responsible for querying data, producing reports, and delivering insights to stakeholders. Analysts are often embedded within business teams and use tools like SQL, Excel, or business intelligence platforms to answer questions. However, they rely on having clean, well-modeled data available to them.

A data engineer is not a data scientist. Data scientists work on developing models, running experiments, and making predictions. Their work is often exploratory and focused on extracting value from data using statistics and machine learning. Yet, before they can experiment or model anything, they need access to high-quality data in the right format, volume, and granularity. This is where data engineers come in.

Data engineers design and manage the systems that make all of this possible. They build reliable data pipelines, maintain data infrastructure, and ensure that data across an organization is trustworthy, scalable, and ready for use [30]. Think of data engineers as railway designers and operators. They build the tracks, switches, and stations that allow cargo (data) to move from one place to another smoothly. If the tracks are poorly laid or the signals fail, trains derail and schedules collapse, just like how analytics and business decisions falter when data pipelines are unreliable.

At first glance, the data engineer may seem distinct from each of these roles. But in practice, they're a hybrid who draws from all of them. They write code with the rigor of a software engineer. They think critically about data access and structure like an analyst. They support experimentation and scalability in the same way a data scientist does. In some cases, they may even find themselves assigned to tasks typically owned by these other roles, depending on the needs of the team. This adaptability is what makes the role so valuable, but also what makes it easy to misunderstand.

So, what is a Data Engineer?

Titles and tools may vary from company to company, but the core responsibilities tend to focus on a few key areas.

First, data engineers build and maintain data pipelines. These are the systems that move data from source systems, such as applications, APIs, or logs, into centralized storage solutions like data warehouses or data lakes. Along the way, the data must be cleaned, structured, and transformed into a format that is usable by others within the organization.

Data engineers are also responsible for managing the infrastructure that supports these pipelines. This can include working with orchestration tools, managing cloud services like AWS Glue or Google Cloud Dataflow, and configuring scalable storage systems such as Snowflake or BigQuery.

Another critical responsibility is maintaining data quality. Engineers build systems to monitor for missing values, schema changes, duplication, and other issues that can affect the reliability of the data. They are often the first to respond when pipelines break or when reports return unexpected results.

Increasingly, data engineers also help define how data is structured and organized. They create models that make data easier to use, more consistent across teams, and more aligned with how the business operates. This modeling work supports everyone who uses data across the company, from analysts to executives.

Foundational Technical Skills

Becoming a data engineer doesn't require you to know everything on day one. Like any technical role, it starts with a foundation and builds over time. Here are the most important skills to focus on, especially if you're just getting started.

1. SQL
   SQL is the language of data. If you want to filter, join, or clean data, this is where you begin. Every data engineer relies on SQL, no matter what tools they use. There are many different dialects of SQL (referred to as SQL flavors), but the core principles remain the same, and learning them provides a transferable skillset across almost any database technology.
2. Programming Languages
   Beyond SQL, a strong data engineer needs to be comfortable with at least one programming language. Python has become the most widely used in the field because of its readability, flexibility, and massive ecosystem of libraries for data manipulation, machine learning, and automation. Over time, depending on the systems your organization uses, you may need to learn additional languages such as Java (common in big data platforms like Hadoop) or Scala (heavily used in Spark). The language itself is less important than the ability to apply it in the context of building reliable, efficient data workflows.
3. Spreadsheets and BI Tools
   Knowing how to explore and visualize data with tools like Excel, Google Sheets, or more sophisticated business intelligence platforms like Tableau, Power BI, or Looker helps you better understand how your data will be consumed. While data engineers do not usually build dashboards, having familiarity with these tools allows you to design pipelines that deliver data in the format and quality that downstream users expect.
4. Database Management
   A data engineer must know how to manage and maintain a database. This includes provisioning, configuring, and monitoring databases, handling indexing and query optimization, and ensuring availability. Familiarity with relational databases

(PostgreSQL, MySQL, SQL Server, Oracle) as well as distributed systems (BigQuery, Snowflake, Redshift) provides the flexibility to handle both transactional and analytical workloads.

5. Schema Modeling

   Engineers must design schemas that balance flexibility and performance, defining tables, relationships, and indexing strategies that make querying efficient and analysis reliable. Knowledge of normalization, star schemas, and snowflake schemas (no relation to Snowflake, the product) helps in building scalable systems that match business needs.

6. Workflow Orchestration

   Modern data pipelines are complex and often span multiple systems. Workflow orchestration is the automated coordination and management of tasks, data, and dependencies to ensure processes run in the correct order, at the right time, and with minimal manual intervention. Tools such as Apache Airflow, Dagster, and Prefect provide scheduling and orchestration capabilities, ensuring that dependencies are respected, tasks are retried on failure, and pipelines can scale reliably with business demand.

7. Cloud Platforms

   Most organizations are shifting data infrastructure to the cloud. A strong data engineer should have familiarity with Amazon Web Services (AWS), Microsoft Azure, or Google Cloud, particularly their storage and compute services such as S3, BigQuery, Redshift, or Azure Synapse. This includes managing permissions, networking, and cost optimization in the cloud environment.

8. Logging, Monitoring, and Alerting

   Skills in setting up logs, dashboards, and alerts using tools such as Prometheus, Grafana, or Elasticsearch, Logstash, Kibana (ELK) stacks ensure that engineers can identify bottlenecks, errors, or outages quickly. Strong monitoring practices reduce downtime and allow proactive issue resolution.

9. Security and Compliance Awareness
   A baseline awareness of data security practices (encryption, secure tunnels, least privilege) and compliance frameworks (GDPR, HIPAA, SOC 2) is essential. Even at the foundational level, a data engineer must know how to handle sensitive data responsibly and securely.

Soft Skills That Matter at Every Level

Technical expertise will get you in the door, but what often determines your impact and how far you can go are the soft skills you bring to the table as with any job.

1. Communication
   You'll often be the bridge between analysts who need reliable datasets, business stakeholders who want insights, and fellow engineers who build the systems. The ability to explain technical concepts in simple, clear terms is one of the most valuable skills you can develop. Good communication prevents misunderstandings, ensures alignment, and makes you a trusted partner in solving organizational problems.
2. Curiosity and Persistence
   The most effective and knowledgeable data engineers are constantly asking questions such as "Why does this number look off?" or "How will this dataset ultimately be used?" They are naturally curious and persistent in chasing down anomalies or inconsistencies. When pipelines break or dashboards show strange results, curiosity leads you to dig deeper, while persistence keeps you from giving up until the issue is understood and fixed.
3. Problem Solving and Creativity
   Things break all the time in data engineering. Pipelines fail, systems run out of resources, and unexpected data formats appear in production. Strong engineers approach these problems with patience, a methodical mindset, and creative thinking. Craftiness often means finding a workaround, reusing a

tool in a new way, or building a small script that saves hours of manual effort. Over time, problem solving becomes one of your most relied-upon skills, shaping how you debug and how you design resilient systems from the start.

4. Collaboration and Empathy

   Competent data engineers recognize that their work directly affects others. Collaboration means listening to the needs of analysts, anticipating the questions data scientists may ask, and working with operations teams to keep systems running smoothly. Empathy helps you understand how your work impacts someone else's success, whether it's an executive making a decision or a student learning from a report.

5. Adaptability

   The tools, frameworks, and practices in data engineering change rapidly. What is cutting-edge today may be outdated in a few years. Adaptability is therefore critical. Engineers who have the ability to embrace change, experiment with new methods, and stay open to feedback are the ones who thrive.

By this point, you've probably realized that being a good data engineer requires more than just memorizing SQL or having the technical know-how to spin up cloud infrastructure. Those skills matter of course, but the real difference comes from how you use them. Your ability to work with people, explain ideas clearly, and make smart trade-offs often matters just as much as the code you write. The technical side gets you in the door, but the soft skills are what make you effective once you're there.

You may feel overwhelmed looking at all of these skills together. That is normal. Few people start with mastery of both technical and soft skills. The important thing is persistence and a willingness to grow. Each new project will strengthen your technical foundation, while every collaboration and every challenge will sharpen your soft skills. Over time, the two will reinforce each other, shaping you into an engineer who can build reliable systems and lead others in doing so.

Your Environment and Equipment

The tools you rely on extend beyond the skills you gain from textbooks and experience. The physical and digital environment you work in plays a major role in how effectively you can design, test, and deliver data solutions.

Computing Power and Workstation Setup

At the core of a data engineer's toolkit is a capable machine. Data engineering often involves processing large datasets, running heavy transformations, and working with virtual environments. While most production work happens in the cloud, a strong local workstation ensures that engineers can prototype, test, and debug efficiently.

A typical setup includes a laptop or desktop with a multi-core processor, at least 16–32 GB of RAM, and fast SSD storage to handle local data files and containerized applications. Dual monitors are also common, as engineers frequently work with multiple windows such as SQL consoles, IDEs, and documentation simultaneously.

Virtualization and Virtual Machines

A virtual machine (VM) is a software-based simulation of a physical computer, running on top of a host machine or cloud infrastructure. VMs can be spun up, configured, and destroyed quickly, making them ideal for testing, experimentation, or scaling workloads without additional hardware. You can access VMs by opening it in software like VirtualBox on your computer or by connecting to it remotely through a login screen from a cloud service.

For data engineers, VMs are invaluable when pipelines need to run in controlled environments. For example, an engineer might create a VM with a specific version of Python, Spark, or Hadoop to replicate production for debugging. Multiple VMs can also run simultaneously, each with different operating systems or configurations, to test compatibility or isolate workloads safely.

The ability to create disposable, customizable environments makes VMs a strong tool to provide flexibility, isolation, and scalability without tying up production systems.

Cloud Infrastructure Access

Modern data engineering depends heavily on cloud services. Engineers rely on cloud resources like VMs, managed databases, and serverless tools to test, deploy, and scale pipelines. Organizations often provide sandbox or staging environments for safe experimentation, while production environments offer the elasticity needed for large-scale data jobs.

Networking and Secure Connections

Because data engineers often connect to remote databases, APIs, and storage services, stable and secure networking equipment is another necessity. VPNs, SSH keys, and sometimes even hardware security tokens may be required to connect securely to enterprise systems. In some companies, engineers use dedicated secure workstations or thin clients that route all traffic through monitored and protected gateways. These tools protect both the engineer and the data they are working with.

Storage Devices and Backup Tools

Even in the cloud era, local and network-attached storage devices remain valuable. Engineers may need external drives for moving large datasets, or backup devices to safeguard scripts and configuration files. On the enterprise side, backup software and snapshot tools ensure that no critical data is lost in the event of a failure. Having both local and cloud-based storage solutions ensures resilience and accessibility.

Development Environment and Accessories

Finally, smaller equipment and accessories also play an important role. High-quality keyboards and ergonomic mice make long coding sessions more comfortable. Noise-canceling headphones are often used for focused work in busy offices. Docking stations, standing desks, and cable management solutions improve ergonomics and workflow efficiency.

Chapter 3

Defining Data 101

"Without data, you're just another person with an opinion."

- W. Edwards [31]

Categorizing Data

Before data can be transformed, analyzed, or visualized, it's important to understand how it's organized. Data comes in many forms. Some of it arrives neatly formatted in rows and columns, while other types come as raw text, messy logs, or loosely structured records. In data engineering, recognizing the differences between structured, semi-structured, and unstructured data is a foundational skill. These categories influence how data is stored, how it can be queried, and how it moves through a pipeline. Just as important is metadata, which provides the context that allows raw data to be interpreted, tracked, and used effectively.

The Three Types of Data

Structured Data is probably what most of us envision when we think of the data that an organization might store. It's characterized by its 'structured' nature as it is formatted in a specific way that makes it understandable and able to be manipulated by humans and machines alike [32].

An easier way of thinking of this data are data points that can be stored in a traditional spreadsheet. For example, a spreadsheet for all schools in the United States could contain columns named Institution Name, City, State, School Level, etc. If we have data elements that can fit into this defined schema, then we have structured data.

Structured data's clarity and ease of manipulation make it ideal for data-driven applications that require clean, consistent inputs. It plays a central role in machine learning, artificial intel-

Boston University	Boston	Massachusetts	University
Queensbury High School	Queensbury	New York	High School
Chinook Middle School	Lacey	Washington	Middle School

Figure 6: Example Structured Data

ligence, business intelligence, and analytics workflows. However, it also comes with limitations. Structured data can be costly to store at scale due to the rigidity of storing information that is fitted into an inflexible schema, may struggle to capture complex or nuanced information, and often lacks the flexibility needed for rapidly changing or irregular data sources. In addition, structured datasets frequently contain missing or incomplete records, which can impact downstream analysis if not handled carefully.

Not all valuable data comes in neat rows and columns. In fact, a vast majority of the world's data is unstructured, meaning it doesn't follow a predefined model or format. For most organizations, unstructured data grows at three times the rate of structured data, meaning that a significant portion of a data engineer's time will be dedicated to working with this data type [33].

This includes everything from raw text files and system logs to scanned documents, emails, audio, video, and images. For example, If we were trying to use unstructured data regarding an academic institution, examples could be district-wide memos, slides used by teachers/professors, and even the school's website itself.

"Homework is due!"

[IMG_2025.jpg]

{audiofile.wav}

Transcript.docx

Figure 7: Example Unstructured Data

While unstructured data is more difficult to work with, it often holds valuable insights, especially in cases where structured data falls short. One of its key advantages is that it captures data in its natural form, allowing it to accommodate information that lacks a predefined structure. Unstructured data is inherently malleable, scalable, and portable, making it suitable for a wide range of use cases. This flexibility naturally leads to lower costs for an organization, as there are more options for the storage of this data.

Many of the issues that arise when using this type of data are caused by the same features that enable its advantages. Its trademark pliability also causes increased complexity when managing and storing this data. It also may be difficult to query for the information you need since there is no SQL counterpart for data without schemas. It also often requires more extensive cleaning and preparation before it becomes usable.

Our third type of data is semi-structured data. Semi-structured data sits between structured and unstructured data. While it doesn't conform to the strict schema of a relational database, it still contains organizational properties that make it easier to parse and interpret than fully unstructured data. It lacks the rigid rows-and-columns format of structured data but includes tags, keys, or metadata that provide context and hierarchy.

Common examples of semi-structured data include JSON, XML, YAML, emails, zipped files, and even some types of binary data. Returning to the school example from earlier, semi-structured data might include email threads between faculty members, JSON files with nested student records, or XML documents that describe library book inventories.

```
{
  "Student": {
    "id": "001",
    "name": "Amy",
    "courses": [
      {"course_id": "CS101", "grade": "A"},
      {"course_id": "MATH210", "grade": "B+"}
    ],
    "email": "amy@example.com"
  }
}
```

Figure 8: Example JSON Semi-Structured Data

Compared to traditional structured data, semi-structured data is more versatile and easier to scale, especially when dealing with varying data formats across systems. Its adaptable nature allows it to integrate more seamlessly with other data sources. It retains the same flexibility when it comes to storage options as its unstructured counterpart. Semi-structured data also often includes metadata or tags, which provide valuable context and can enhance the depth and quality of downstream analysis.

However, it also inherits some of the challenges of unstructured data, like increased complexity in storage and management, as well as limited querying capabilities compared to fully structured relational databases.

In many cases, data engineers will transform semi-structured data into structured form to make it easier to query, join, and analyze using standard tools. But, semi-structured data can also be used directly in modern platforms. JSON, XML, and Avro are often stored in cloud data lakes, streamed through event pipelines, or queried natively in systems like Snowflake, BigQuery, and MongoDB. This flexibility allows teams to strike a balance between structure and adaptability, depending on the needs of the pipeline.

The Role of Metadata

Metadata is often described as "data about data," but that simple definition doesn't fully capture its importance. In practice, metadata provides the context that makes raw data meaningful. It helps systems and humans interpret, organize, and manage information, especially when working with semi-structured and unstructured formats where structure is either flexible or completely absent.

Think of metadata like the label on a file folder in a filing cabinet. The contents inside the folder are your actual data. But without the label, you wouldn't know what the folder contains, who it belongs to, when it was filed, or whether it's even relevant to what you're looking for.

Metadata is that label. It doesn't contain the main content, but it tells you what the data is, where it came from, when it was created, and how to use it. Just like you wouldn't want to search through dozens of unlabeled folders, modern data systems rely on metadata to quickly organize, access, and make sense of large volumes of raw information.

Metadata also plays a crucial role in organizations that seek to keep costs low on data storage and management. Gartner, an American research and advisory firm, found that enterprises that don't take a metadata-driven approach to IT modernization can spend as much as 40% more on data management [34].


```
{
 "name": "file.ext",
 "type": "dataset",
 "created_at": "YYYY-MM-DD",
 "owner": "user@example.com",
 "size": 12345,
 "fields": ["id", "date", "value"],
 "tags": ["example", "sample"]
}
```


Figure 9: Simple Metadata

Metadata is also essential in lineage tracking and auditing. Knowing how data was generated, transformed, and used across different systems helps teams trace any issues that may arise down the line, meet compliance requirements, and avoid inevitable data drift specifically in machine learning workflows.

Data drift, in short, occurs when the data flowing into a machine learning model in production begins to differ from the data it was originally trained on. When this happens, the model becomes obsolete over time because it's no longer aligned with current trends, user behavior, or external conditions. As a result, its predictions may become inaccurate, misleading, or even harmful depending on the application [35]. In this context, metadata plays an important role. By tracking input distributions, feature statistics, and model performance over time, metadata helps engineers detect drift early and understand where and why it may be happening.

Databases and Data Stores

Before we can talk about pipelining, it's important to understand the systems that hold data. Data engineers pull from a wide variety of sources, each with its own design philosophy and trade-offs. At the heart of this ecosystem are databases and data stores, two broad categories that often get used interchangeably, but which serve different purposes. Knowing the differences, and when to use each, is critical for building efficient and reliable data pipelines.

A database is typically designed for structured information and governed by a schema. Relational databases such as PostgreSQL, MySQL, or Oracle organize data into tables, enforce constraints, and excel at transactional workloads where accuracy and consistency are paramount like tracking bank balances, hospital records, or order histories. These systems usually power operational applications and prioritize ACID properties (Atomicity, Consistency, Isolation, Durability) to ensure reliability [36].

A data store, by contrast, is a broader category that includes systems designed for more flexible or specialized use cases. This might mean storing semi-structured JSON in MongoDB, persisting massive volumes of unstructured logs in a data lake like Amazon S3, or caching session data in an in-memory system like Redis. Data stores often relax schema and consistency requirements in exchange for speed, scalability, or cost savings. They are optimized for particular access patterns such as key-value lookups, document retrieval, or graph traversals.

The distinction matters because the extraction process depends heavily on the source system. Pulling from a transactional database typically involves structured queries, while working with a data store may require handling unstructured files, streaming events, or semi-structured objects. Databases shine when consistency and reliability are essential, while data stores thrive when flexibility and scale are the priority.

Relational Database Management Systems (RDBMS)

Relational databases remain the backbone of most business systems. They organize data into tables made up of rows and columns, with each table representing a specific entity such as customers, orders, or employees. The "relational" aspect comes from linking these tables through keys, allowing for complex queries across datasets. Structured Query Language (SQL) is the standard way to interact with these systems, making them both powerful and accessible for analysts, developers, and data engineers alike.

Examples of relational databases include PostgreSQL, MySQL, Oracle Database, and Microsoft SQL Server. PostgreSQL is often praised for its open-source flexibility and advanced features like JSON support and window functions, making it a go-to choice for modern applications. MySQL powers countless websites and web applications thanks to its simplicity and strong community support. Oracle and SQL Server, on the other hand, dominate in large enterprises where scale, performance, and commercial support are non-negotiable. Despite differences in features and licensing, all of these systems follow the same core relational principles.

One of the defining strengths of relational databases is their adherence to ACID properties—Atomicity, Consistency, Isolation, and Durability as mentioned before [36]. This means that every transaction, whether it's transferring money between two bank accounts or updating a patient's medical record, is guaranteed to be executed reliably and safely. For industries where accuracy is paramount, for example, in finance, healthcare, government, this reliability is critical. A bank cannot risk misplacing a transaction, just as a hospital cannot risk losing a lab result.

Relational databases are best suited for transactional workloads or Online Transaction Processing (OLTP). This includes any system where lots of small, concurrent reads and writes need to be handled quickly and consistently. For example, an e-commerce platform might use a relational database to track orders and payments, ensuring that inventory counts remain correct even when thousands of customers are shopping at once. Similarly, a university might rely on a relational database to manage student enrollment, making sure that no more than 30 students are registered for a class with a strict capacity.

However, relational databases are not a one-size-fits-all solution. While they excel at structured, transactional data, they struggle with massive volumes of semi-structured or unstructured data such as logs, clickstreams, or video files. For that, organizations often turn to other types of data stores like NoSQL databases or data lakes. Still, relational databases remain the gold standard when the use case demands consistency, structure, and reliability.

NoSQL Datastores

While relational databases dominate traditional business applications, not all data fits neatly into rows and columns. That's where NoSQL datastores come in. The term "NoSQL" doesn't mean "no SQL ever," but rather "not only SQL" [37]. These systems are designed to handle more flexible, large-scale, or specialized workloads that relational databases often struggle with. They generally trade strict schemas and strong consistency for scalability, availability, and speed, making them especially popular in modern web, mobile, and IoT applications.

One of the most common types of NoSQL databases is the document store, with MongoDB being the best-known example. Instead of tables, data is stored as documents, often in a JSON-like format that can vary in structure. This flexibility is a huge advantage for applications where new fields are added frequently or records don't all follow the same pattern. For example, an e-commerce catalog might have one product with size and color attributes, while another product has entirely different fields like engine type or warranty period. With a document store, both can be stored side by side without schema changes.

Another major category is the key-value store, which maps unique keys to values for extremely fast lookups. Systems like Redis and Amazon DynamoDB are widely used when speed is critical, such as caching web sessions, storing user preferences, or managing leaderboards in gaming applications. Because they're optimized for simple queries, they can serve millions of requests per second with low latency, making them ideal for high-traffic, real-time systems.

For large-scale analytical and time-series data, wide-column stores like Apache Cassandra and HBase offer another flavor of NoSQL. These systems distribute data across many servers and are designed to handle massive volumes of writes and reads. Social media platforms, for example, often rely on Cassandra to track billions of posts, likes, and comments in real time, ensuring that activity feeds can be updated instantly as users interact with the system.

Finally, there are graph databases, such as Neo4j or Amazon Neptune, which specialize in modeling relationships between entities. Instead of tables or documents, data is stored as nodes and edges, making them ideal for use cases like fraud detection, social networks, or recommendation engines. For instance, a graph database can quickly find patterns asking, "Which customers know each other and bought the same product," something that would be extremely cumbersome to query in a relational system.

NoSQL datastores are not a replacement for relational databases. Rather, you can view them as a natural complement to relational databases. Their strength lies in flexibility, horizontal scalability, and support for unstructured or semi-structured data. Though, they often lack the strong transactional guarantees and mature tooling of relational systems. As a result, they're best suited for workloads where scalability and speed matter more than strict consistency, and where data doesn't need to follow a rigid schema.

Data Lakes

While databases and NoSQL datastores are designed to serve applications or transactional systems, data lakes are built to store raw, large-scale datasets in their native format. Instead of enforcing a schema when data is written, data lakes follow a schema-on-read philosophy: you can dump almost anything in, and decide how to interpret it later. This makes them ideal for organizations that deal with huge, diverse, or rapidly changing data sources, since they don't need to preprocess everything before storage.

Examples of data lake technologies include Amazon S3, Azure Data Lake Storage, and Google Cloud Storage. These systems can handle petabytes of structured, semi-structured, and unstructured data, everything from CSV files and JSON logs to images, videos, and IoT sensor streams. For instance, a media company might use a data lake to store raw video footage alongside viewer interaction logs, while a pharmaceutical company might store genetic sequencing data next to clinical trial results. Because the lake doesn't impose a rigid schema, both structured and unstructured data can coexist in the same store.

The flexibility of data lakes also makes them attractive for machine learning and advanced analytics. Data scientists often want access to the rawest possible form of the data, without transformations that may have stripped away useful detail. A retail company, for example, could use its data lake to hold both raw transaction logs and clickstream data, then run feature engineering directly on the raw files before training recommendation models. Similarly, a financial firm might use a data lake to capture years of tick-level trading data, enabling research into new algorithms without having to remodel historical records.

However, the same flexibility that makes data lakes powerful can also make them risky. Without strong governance, they can devolve into what's often called a "data swamp"—a messy collection of files with little documentation or organization, making it difficult to find or trust the data later [38]. Data lakes are best used when scale and variety are the priorities. They don't replace databases or NoSQL stores, but they provide a long-term home for data that may not yet have a defined use case. By capturing everything in its raw form, organizations ensure they have the flexibility to analyze it later as new questions and opportunities arise.

Data Warehouses

If data lakes are about storing raw information in all its messy variety, data warehouses are about providing a clean, structured environment where that information can be turned into actionable insights. A data warehouse is a central repository optimized for analytical workloads or Online Analytical Processing (OLAP) rather than transactional workloads (OLTP). Instead of focusing on small, frequent updates like a relational database, warehouses are designed for large, complex queries that summarize, aggregate, and analyze millions or billions of rows at once.

Classic on-premises data warehouses include Teradata, Oracle Exadata, and IBM Netezza, which were widely used in enterprises long before the cloud era. More recently, cloud-native systems like Snowflake, Google BigQuery, and Amazon Redshift have redefined what warehouses can do. These platforms offer near-infinite scalability, elastic compute, and cost models based on usage rather than fixed infrastructure. For example, BigQuery allows analysts to run petabyte-scale SQL queries in seconds without managing servers, while Snowflake's architecture separates storage from compute, enabling multiple teams to query the same data without stepping on each other's toes.

One of the key strengths of data warehouses is their columnar storage format, which allows for highly efficient analytical queries. Instead of reading entire rows of data, warehouses can scan only the specific columns required for a query, drastically reducing I/O.

Data warehouses are also where concepts like star schemas, fact and dimension tables, and business intelligence modeling come into play. A retail company, for instance, might maintain a sales fact table recording every transaction, linked to dimensions such as product, customer, and time. Analysts can then slice and dice this information to see sales by region, product category, or customer demographic. Because the data has already been cleaned and modeled before entering the warehouse (in traditional ETL pipelines), users can trust that the metrics they query are reliable.

Data Marts

While data warehouses serve as the central hub for an organization's analytical data, not every team needs access to the full warehouse or the ability to query across every domain. That's where data marts come in. A data mart is essentially a subset of a data warehouse, focused on a specific business unit, department, or function. Instead of providing enterprise-wide data, a mart delivers curated datasets tailored to the needs of a particular audience or department.

For example, a large retailer might have a central data warehouse storing everything from sales transactions and customer information to supplier records and inventory levels. The marketing team, however, may only care about customer demographics, campaign performance, and purchase histories. By creating a marketing data mart, the organization can provide marketers with just the data they need, structured in a way that aligns with their workflows, without exposing them to the complexity or cost of querying the full warehouse.

Data marts can be built in different ways. In some organizations, they are dependent data marts, created as slices of an existing warehouse to maintain consistency with enterprise-wide data definitions like Inmon's top-down approach. In other cases, they are independent data marts, built directly from source systems for quicker delivery, echoing Kimball's bottom-up approach we also discussed earlier [39]. The choice between the two ultimately comes down to the same trade-offs already outlined: consistency and governance on one side, versus speed and flexibility on the other.

In-Memory Stores

While databases, warehouses, and lakes are designed to persist data for long-term use, sometimes the priority is speed above all else. That's where in-memory data stores come in. These systems keep data in main memory rather than disk, making reads and writes orders of magnitude faster. Instead of holding petabytes of historical data, they are designed to serve small, frequently accessed datasets where latency must be measured in milliseconds or microseconds.

The most widely used in-memory store is Redis, an open-source system that supports simple key-value pairs as well as more advanced data structures like lists, sets, and sorted sets. Redis is often used as a cache layer in front of a slower database or API, storing session information, user preferences, or frequently queried results so they can be retrieved instantly [40]. For example, a social media app might cache a user's news feed in Redis so that refreshing the feed feels instantaneous, even though building it from scratch requires many complex queries in the background.

Another common option is Memcached, a lightweight caching system designed specifically for key-value lookups. It's especially popular for web applications that need to scale horizontally and serve millions of requests quickly. While Redis has become the more feature-rich option, Memcached still enables caching at companies like Meta, where ultra-low latency matters more than advanced data structures [41].

In-memory stores are also used for real-time analytics and event-driven systems. For instance, financial trading platforms may use them to track live market data, where every microsecond counts. Gaming platforms often use Redis leaderboards to update player rankings in real time, while IoT applications may temporarily buffer streaming sensor data in memory before pushing it to a warehouse or lake for long-term storage.

The trade-offs are important to note. Because these systems store data in memory, they are constrained by RAM size, making them more expensive and less suitable for very large datasets. Persistence options exist like how Redis can write snapshots to disk, but the main use case remains ephemeral, fast-moving data rather than permanent storage.

In-memory stores play a supporting role in the data ecosystem. They complement databases and warehouses by providing caching, acceleration, and real-time responsiveness. When designed well, they ensure that end users experience smooth, instant interactions, even when the underlying systems are complex and heavy.

Other Specialized Data Stores

Beyond relational databases, NoSQL systems, data lakes,

warehouses, marts, and in-memory caches, the data ecosystem includes a wide range of other specialized data stores. These systems are often built for niche workloads or to solve very specific problems that don't fit neatly into the categories we've already covered. While you may not encounter them every day, it's important to be aware of their existence, as they can appear in extraction workflows depending on the industry or use case.

One example is time-series databases such as InfluxDB, TimescaleDB, or Prometheus, which are optimized for data that changes over time like metrics, logs, sensor readings, or financial ticks. These systems can efficiently ingest, compress, and query billions of timestamped events, making them popular in monitoring, IoT, and fintech applications.

Another specialized category is search engines like Elasticsearch, OpenSearch, and Apache Solr, which double as data stores optimized for full-text search and log analytics. Instead of focusing on relational joins or aggregations, they're built to quickly retrieve documents that match keywords, filters, or relevance scores. Companies often use them to power search boxes on websites, monitor logs in real time, or analyze machine data from servers and applications.

Finally, there are file systems and distributed stores that blur the lines between data storage and infrastructure. Systems like the Hadoop Distributed File System (HDFS) or Ceph provide low-level building blocks for data lakes and large-scale analytics platforms. Data storage architectures that manage data as discrete units called objects AKA object stores (MinIO, Backblaze B2), offer cloud-like storage semantics for organizations running private or hybrid environments.

These "other" stores highlight the diversity of the data landscape. Each was created to solve a specific problem: scaling time-series metrics, enabling fast text search, modeling graphs, or distributing massive file collections. The key is not to memorize every possible technology but to recognize the patterns.

Ask: Is this data primarily relational? Time-based? Text-heavy? Relationship-driven? Raw files? The answer will point you toward the type of store most likely to appear in your pipeline and shape the way you design your ETL process.

Chapter 4

Fundamentals of Modern Data Pipelining

"The only way to go fast, is to go well."

– Robert C. Martin [42]

An Overview of Data Pipelining

In the world of data engineering, there are very few concepts that are as foundational as ETL and ELT pipelining. These two approaches, which stand for Extract → Transform → Load and Extract → Load → Transform respectively, are data integration processes that combine, normalize, and organize raw datasets from a variety of sources into a single, consistent, format. This unified data set is then stored (written to disk) in a target data store such as a data warehouse or another staging area. Staging areas (or landing zones) are intermediate storage locations for the temporary storage of integrated data. These are often transient in nature, which means that the data that they temporarily house are erased after data extraction is complete. However, this data may also be kept to preserve history. These are known as persistent storage areas.

In this chapter, we will begin by taking a closer look at ETL, which is the more traditional and still widely used approach to data integration. While newer architectures like ELT have become more popular in cloud-native environments, ETL is still deeply embedded in many enterprise systems and continues to support pipelines across a wide range of industries.

Extraction

Every data pipeline begins with one fundamental question: where is the data coming from? The extract phase is all about answering that question. Extraction refers to the process of pulling raw data from its original source systems so that it can be processed downstream. Let's explore some of the source systems that you should be familiar with while working on this step in the ETL pipeline.

Application Programming Interfaces (APIs)

Application Programming Interfaces or APIs for short is the protocol used for communication between two software applications. It might be useful to envision that APIs are a 'bridge' that connects two separate systems, and lets them share data and services between them. While there are many ways to design and utilize APIs, the most common approach follows the HTTP protocol, where applications send and receive data through standardized web requests.

In HTTP-based APIs, specific endpoints are exposed that act as access points for these requests. These endpoints are often managed through an API Gateway, which handles incoming traffic and routes it to the appropriate backend service or resource.

APIs are one of the most common ways that data engineers extract data, in part because they offer an intuitive and widely used method for accessing information. Nearly every modern software platform exposes data through APIs in some form. For example, Snapchat's API can provide aggregated user engagement metrics, Shopify's API can return order and inventory details from an online store, and Stripe's API allows access to transaction histories and customer payment information [43], [44]. These systems provide structured endpoints that data engineers can query to retrieve valuable data for analysis and reporting. APIs as a data source can offer incremental, real-time data access for dashboards, easy-to-use and structured data models, strong integration capabilities across platforms, built-in scalability, and robust security features that simplify access control and compliance.

APIs can be broadly divided into internal and external types. Internal APIs operate within an organization, connecting systems such as HR and payroll or linking customer databases to analytics tools. They simplify integration while keeping data secure inside the company. External APIs, by contrast, are exposed to partners, customers, or third-party developers. These include payment processors, logistics providers, weather services, and social media platforms. External APIs can enrich internal datasets with context such as financial transactions, delivery statuses, or demographic trends, but they also bring stricter access policies, rate limits, and sometimes licensing costs.

There are also some challenges that come with using APIs that data engineers should be aware of. For example, many APIs restrict how often they can be called within a certain time frame, a limitation known as rate limiting. Additionally, the very features that make APIs secure such as authentication keys, tokens, or permission scopes, can also make them more complex to access and maintain.

Relational Databases

In addition to serving as common destinations in ETL workflows as we touched on before, relational databases are also one of the most widely used sources of data. Typically, a data engineer might interact and glean data from this source using SQL queries. To do so, they may employ a few different tools like the Java Database Connectivity (JDBC) protocol. JDBC is a Java-based API that enables applications to connect to and interact with these databases. It allows engineers to define SQL queries within Java programs in order to retrieve, update, and manipulate data stored in the target database [45].

Another tool in a similar vein to JDBC is the Open Database Connectivity (ODBC) API. ODBC is a more language-agnostic and environment-flexible alternative, allowing engineers to query relational databases using languages such as Python, C, .NET, and others. Like JDBC, it enables applications to connect to and interact with RDBMS platforms, but it's better suited for non-Java environments and is widely supported by data analysis tools and business intelligence platforms [46], [47].

The scripts that you write using these tools can be scheduled to run at different frequencies and at times of your choosing. This allows you to extract data on a set schedule, often daily, hourly, or even every few minutes depending on the needs of the business. Scheduled extractions are optimal with batch processing pipelines, since the chunks are simply data from a specific time frame. They are especially effective when paired with incremental extraction strategies, where only the data that has changed since the last run is retrieved. This is often done by filtering on a column such as last_updated, which tracks the most recent modification timestamp for each row.

While timestamp-based incremental extraction is effective,

it depends on consistent update logic and accurate timestamps within the source tables. In practice, this can be error-prone or incomplete. Change Data Capture (CDC), offers a more robust solution by tracking and capturing data changes at the database level. Rather than relying on application logic or specific query filters, CDC monitors inserts, updates, and deletes directly from the database's internal logs or system tables [48]. This ensures a more accurate and complete picture of what changed, when it changed, and how. Many modern RDBMS systems like Azure SQL Database, AWS SQL Server, and Oracle, offer built-in CDC features or extensions that allow engineers to stream changes as they happen or retrieve them as part of scheduled batch jobs.

Like APIs, RDBMS platforms provide data engineers with access to structured data (in the forms of columns and rows). It also provides an easy way to interface with them using common programming languages and tools.

Flat Files

Flat files can also be strong data sources, especially in organizations that rely on spreadsheets or manual data exports. These files typically store data in a simple, tabular format such as CSV, TSV, or Excel, where each row represents a record and each column corresponds to a field. Because they are easy to generate, view, and share, flat files are often used for ad hoc reporting, external data exchange, and lightweight integrations.

In modern data pipelines, the extraction of flat files is often automated to eliminate manual effort and ensure timely data processing. Rather than waiting for someone to trigger a job manually, data engineers set up file watchers or event-based triggers to monitor directories or storage locations for new files. For example, in cloud environments like AWS, when a flat file is uploaded to an S3 bucket, a trigger (such as an S3 event notification) can invoke an AWS Lambda function or start an AWS Glue job. Similarly, in Google Cloud Platform (GCP), a new file in Google Cloud Storage can trigger a Cloud Function to begin the extraction process. In more traditional environments, engineers might use cron jobs or orchestration tools like Apache Airflow to periodically scan a network drive or SFTP location for new files.

Once a file is detected, the extraction script reads it using appropriate tools, the pandas Python library or csv modules for CSVs, openpyxl or xlrd Python libraries for Excel files, and json libraries for JSON formats. Metadata such as file name, upload timestamp, and expected schema can also be logged to track what was picked up and prevent reprocessing. This automated detection and extraction framework ensures that pipelines are both repeatable and scalable, even when the flat files come from manual or third-party sources.

Event Streaming Tools

Platforms like Apache Kafka are designed to process data in real time and thrive within event-driven architectures. In today's connected world, billions of data sources are constantly generating events, that is, discrete pieces of information that represent something that happened. These events could be anything from placing an online food order, submitting a web form, or an IoT sensor sending a reading from a wind park. Event streaming platforms allow developers to build systems that ingest, process and make decisions on data as it arrives while also maintaining the order and reliability of every event.

So how does Kafka enable all of this functionality? It begins with a core design pattern known as the publish-subscribe (pub-sub) architecture. In this model, one or more producers write data to Kafka topics (publishing events into a distributed log). On the other end, consumers subscribe to those topics and read the events in the order they were written. This decoupling between producers and consumers allows for high scalability and fault-tolerance: multiple consumers can read the same stream independently, and Kafka ensures the data is not lost even in the event of failure.

To extract data from Kafka, data engineers use consumer applications that subscribe to specific topics. These consumers read the stream of incoming events as they arrive, often using libraries like Kafka's native client or higher-level frameworks such as Kafka Streams or Spark Structured Streaming. The consumer tracks its position in the stream using offsets, which makes it possible to resume from where it left off in the event of a failure. This flexibility allows engineers to process real-time data or reprocess historical events if needed.

In many production environments, the extracted events are passed directly into transformation logic or routed into another system for storage, such as a data warehouse, a database, or cloud object storage. This makes Kafka a powerful choice for building pipelines that need to move large volumes of data continuously and reliably [49].

While Apache Kafka has been open sourced and free-to-use since 2011 when it was donated to the Apache Software Foundation, several enterprise platforms have been built around it to offer managed infrastructure, monitoring, security, and simplified development. Whether you are working in a real-time analytics environment or building data pipelines that require low latency and high reliability, becoming familiar with event streaming platforms like Kafka and its managed counterparts is a valuable skill for any data engineer during the Extraction stage of ETL.

One of the most notable platforms built on top of Kafka is Confluent, a modern data streaming solution created by the original developers of Apache Kafka. Confluent offers a fully managed Kafka service along with a suite of tools for elastic scalability, robust security, and seamless integration with cloud providers. Designed to be cloud-native and serverless, Confluent can be deployed in any environment and manages infrastructure automatically through fully managed clusters. Compared to self-managed Kafka deployments, Confluent provides enhanced monitoring, schema management, and enterprise-grade security features [50].

Other cloud providers such as AWS MSK, Azure Event Hubs, and Google Cloud's Pub/Sub offer managed Kafka-compatible services to reduce operational overhead for teams that want Kafka's capabilities without managing infrastructure.

Web Scraping

Web scraping is the algorithmic extraction of information from the web (hence, the name web scraping). While a human could manually copy and paste information, typically, the term refers to using software that automates this process. This software can systematically navigate websites, identify relevant content, and extract data such as text, images, or links. The scraped data is often saved as structured data, but can also be left as unstructured or semi-structured data as well.

To do this efficiently, data engineers often rely on a range of popular tools and libraries. BeautifulSoup is commonly used for parsing HTML and XML content, especially when working with static web pages. For more dynamic sites that rely heavily on JavaScript, tools like Selenium or Playwright can automate browser interactions and capture content that wouldn't be accessible through simple HTTP requests. These would be used manually by the data engineer in relatively simple scripts that are run for relatively small datasets.

For large-scale or production-grade scraping, frameworks like Scrapy offer built-in support for asynchronous crawling, data pipelines, and robust error handling. These tools help engineers quickly collect and prepare web data as a valuable input source for analytics or machine learning workflows.

Surveys and Forms

Surveys and forms represent another valuable source of data for data engineers. Unlike APIs or flat files that are often generated automatically by systems, survey and form data comes directly from human input. This can make it especially useful for capturing subjective information such as opinions, preferences, or feedback that may not exist anywhere else in structured systems.

Common scenarios are companies distributing employee satisfaction surveys or surveys sent out to customers through a tool like Google Forms, Typeform, or SurveyMonkey. The responses often include both structured fields (multiple choice, ratings, dropdowns) and unstructured fields (open-ended text responses). This creates an interesting challenge: extracting both the clean tabular data and the free-form text that may require additional processing, such as natural language analysis or categorization.

Most survey platforms allow data exports in formats like CSV, JSON, or Excel. This makes them compatible with pipelines that can automatically ingest files dropped into a cloud storage bucket or downloaded via an API connection. Some platforms, such as Google Forms, also integrate directly with Google Sheets, which provides a continuously updated data source that can be connected to downstream ETL processes.

The main benefit of survey and form data is its direct connection to end users or stakeholders, capturing the "voice" of those interacting with a product or service. However, this also introduces risks such as missing responses, inconsistent formatting, or biased sampling.

When managed carefully, survey and form data can enrich organizational datasets with unique insights that cannot be gleaned from purely transactional or system-generated records. It often plays a supporting role in analytics projects, such as customer feedback analysis, employee engagement tracking, or academic research studies.

Videos

Extracting data from videos usually means working with either the audio track, the frames of the video, or the metadata (timestamps, titles, subtitles, etc.). For example, YouTube provides APIs that can give you structured metadata about videos, comments, and captions [51]. When APIs are available, data engineers can use tools like FFmpeg to extract frames or audio, and then apply further processing such as speech-to-text transcription for spoken content or object detection on frames using machine learning models. This type of extraction is often used in areas like media analytics, customer sentiment tracking from recorded calls, or surveillance video analysis.

Images

Images hold vast amounts of unstructured data. The extraction process may involve Optical Character Recognition (OCR) to pull text from images using tools like Apache's Tesseract OCR or computer vision models to detect objects, classify scenes, or tag entities within images. For example, an e-commerce site may scrape product images and run them through an image classification model to automatically categorize products. Metadata embedded in image files (EXIF data like timestamps, GPS coordinates, or device type) can also be extracted to provide useful context.

PDFs

PDFs are a very common source of business data. Think invoices, contracts, research papers, or reports. The challenge is that PDFs often store data in a visually formatted way rather than a structured table. Tools like PDFMiner, PyPDF2, or Apache Tika can extract raw text, while libraries like Camelot or Tabula are tailored for extracting structured tables from PDFs. Engineers may need to combine text parsing with metadata extraction (such as author, date, or embedded keywords) to make sense of the information.

Other Document Types

Beyond PDFs, data engineers often encounter Word documents and PowerPoint slides. These can be extracted using libraries like python-docx, and python-pptx respectively. Logs and emails are another frequent unstructured source, where tools like IMAP libraries or log parsing frameworks are used. The key challenge is always converting these irregular formats into something structured enough to integrate into a data pipeline.

Pre-Extraction Considerations

Before any data leaves its source system, a data engineer has to pause and plan. Rushing into it without proper forethought can result in wasted effort, unnecessary costs, or even regulatory trouble.

The first step is scoping requirements. A well-designed

extraction job should pull only what is needed, nothing more and nothing less. For example, if a marketing team only needs click-stream data for the past three months, it makes little sense to extract the full five-year history of web logs. Pulling too much data increases processing time and storage costs while pulling too little leaves analysts and stakeholders without the answers they need.

Next comes data profiling, where engineers quickly assess what the source system looks like. This might involve running sample queries, checking row counts, looking at column data types, or inspecting whether certain fields contain missing or inconsistent values. A short profiling phase often prevents larger issues later, such as discovering mid-pipeline that a "date" field actually contains free-form text entries.

Finally, and perhaps most importantly, there are legal and compliance checks. Different types of data come with different obligations. Personally identifiable information (PII) may be governed by GDPR in Europe or CCPA in California. Health-related data could fall under HIPAA in the United States. Even financial transaction data may require specific encryption or access restrictions. Before any extraction is scheduled, engineers must confirm that pulling and moving the data will not create compliance violations. In some cases, this may require consultation with legal or compliance teams to get approval. We will cover this extensively in a later section.

By carefully scoping, profiling, and ensuring compliance before extraction, engineers set the stage for smoother pipelines and fewer unpleasant surprises downstream. Pre-extraction planning may feel like a slowdown, but it's an investment that pays off many times over once the pipeline is running in production.

Finding Data and Identifying Applicable Sources

One of the earliest and most important steps in a project is figuring out where the data actually lives. While it may sound obvious, locating the right sources can be tricky, especially in large organizations or when working with external partners. A well-designed extraction strategy starts with knowing what data is available and evaluating whether it is useful for your goals.

1. Start with the business problem.
   The first tip is to let the problem guide your search. If the task is to understand customer churn, the most relevant sources might be your CRM system, customer support logs, and subscription records. If you are analyzing supply chain efficiency, the useful data may come from inventory databases, vendor files, and logistics APIs. For a meal-kit delivery company, this means focusing on data about cancellations, delivery histories, and support tickets, rather than pulling every dataset in sight. By working backward from the business question, you avoid collecting data just for the sake of having it.
2. Look internally before going external.
   Many organizations already generate more data than they use. Before investing in third-party datasets, survey what is already available. Check with teams like marketing, finance, sales, or IT to learn what systems and reports they maintain. You may discover that some of the data you need is sitting unused in a warehouse, spreadsheet, or archived system. In our meal-kit example, those two internal sources already provide valuable churn insights without the need to purchase external data.
3. Map systems and stakeholders.
   A practical step is to create a map of the systems in use across the organization and the stakeholders responsible for them. This can help you identify where data might reside and who can provide access or context. Building these relationships early prevents bottlenecks later when you need approvals or explanations of how the data is generated. For the meal-kit company, this might mean documenting that sales owns the CRM, product owns the subscription database, and operations owns the delivery logs. Building these relationships early prevents bottlenecks when you need approvals or clarification on how the data is generated.

4. Use external public datasets when appropriate.
   In addition to internal systems, many governments, universities, and research institutions publish free datasets. Platforms like data.gov (U.S. government data), Kaggle, or the World Bank Open Data can provide rich context that complements your internal sources. A churn analysis may benefit from adding U.S. Census demographics by region, which could reveal that cancellations are higher in areas with younger, more transient populations.
5. Evaluate accessibility and quality.
   For every source, determining whether it's accessible and reliable is a requirement. Does the system provide an API or export function, or will it require a custom scraping solution? Is the data regularly updated, or is it stale? Does it contain complete, accurate records, or are there gaps that could compromise your analysis? These questions help you prioritize the most effective sources. In the meal-kit scenario, CRM exports may arrive daily in clean CSVs, while delivery data must be pulled from an API that sometimes lags, a limitation that needs to be documented so stakeholders know it is not truly real-time.
6. Stay curious and keep learning.
   Finally, cultivating curiosity is key. Talk to people outside your immediate team, explore the tools your organization already pays for, and stay current on industry news. New data sources are constantly emerging, from IoT devices to third-party SaaS integrations. A curious data engineer might discover that delivery trucks record temperature and transit times, raising a new hypothesis: poor delivery conditions could be contributing to churn. Insights like this often come from curiosity as much as from formal system maps.

Common Pitfalls in the Extract Stage

After covering the fundamentals, it helps to name the issues that most often derail extraction in real projects. A frequent misstep is overloading source systems: heavy, recurring queries against production during business hours can throttle application performance and frustrate end users. Even when load is manageable, extracts can be incomplete or inconsistent. Jobs that fail mid-run, queries that miss late-arriving records, or repeated runs that capture slightly different snapshots will all seed downstream discrepancies.

Incremental logic is another fragile spot. Without careful design, you get duplicates or missed updates. Timestamp filters can go awry with clock drift or irregular update logging, and CDC can fail when logs are purged before readers catch up. Weak error handling multiplies the risk. Unhandled network issues, API rate limits, or corrupted files can cause silent failures that only surface when dashboards show gaps. Finally, schema drift at the source can break extraction scripts. Renamed fields, changed types, or altered tables may quietly produce partial or malformed datasets if no one detects the change.

Best Practices in the Extract Stage

To avoid these traps, start by minimizing load on sources. Schedule pulls for off-peak windows, rely on read replicas, and respect API rate limits with smaller, incremental requests. Prefer incremental extraction over full reloads. Techniques like timestamps, CDC, or log-based replication reduce cost and contention while focusing on actual changes. Because issues still occur, build robust monitoring. Track failures, latency, and volume anomalies, and alert on them so problems are caught before they propagate. Validate early and automatically. Use row counts, schema checks, and quick profiles of nulls, ranges, and uniqueness to stop bad data at the door.

Expect schema drift and plan for it with automated detection and comparison tooling. Either adapt the pipeline or raise clear flags so engineers can intervene quickly. Preserve raw extracts in a staging area to provide an audit trail and to enable painless reprocessing if downstream steps fail. Finally, treat extraction logic like production software. Document it, version-control it, and keep filters, schedules, and assumptions visible and reviewable as the system evolves.

Together, these practices turn extraction from a brittle chore into a dependable foundation. They protect source systems, shorten recovery time when incidents occur, and feed the transform and load stages with data you can trust.

Transform

Once data has been successfully extracted from its source, it rarely arrives in a format that is ready to be analyzed or directly consumed by end users. Raw data often contains inconsistencies, errors, missing values, or structures that are misaligned across systems. This is where the transformation step comes in. Transformation is the process of cleaning, reshaping, and enriching data so that it can support analysis, reporting, or machine learning.

Transformation is often the most labor-intensive stage of the data pipeline. Data engineers spend a significant portion of their time here because messy, inconsistent data is the norm rather than the exception. Think of transformation as the act of smelting iron ore into iron ingots. Without it, the information sitting in your warehouse or lake would be difficult to query and unreliable to act on.

This step can involve a wide range of activities. At the most basic level, it includes correcting errors, removing duplicates, and filling in missing values. At a higher level, it means normalizing data so that fields are comparable across systems, standardizing formats such as dates or currencies, or deriving new features that better capture the meaning of the data. In some cases, transformation also involves aggregating massive datasets into summaries that are easier to analyze.

Transformation is also where business logic and domain knowledge get encoded. For example, the way a company defines "active users," "revenue," or "customer churn" must be captured and consistently applied in transformation scripts. By doing so, data engineers ensure that everyone in the organization is speaking the same language and making decisions on the same definitions.

Finally, transformation has an important role in governance

and compliance. Sensitive data that you have extracted might need to be masked, anonymized, or redacted to meet legal requirements. Audit trails must be preserved to show how data moved from one state to another. A well-designed transformation process doesn't just prepare data for analysis, it also ensures that the data remains trustworthy, compliant, and aligned with organizational needs.

Filtering

Filtering is often the very first transformation applied to raw data. Not all extracted data is useful, and sometimes including everything in the pipeline only increases cost, storage, and noise. Filtering ensures that only relevant records make it into downstream systems.

For structured data, such as relational databases, filtering might mean applying conditions like WHERE clauses in SQL queries to select rows that meet certain criteria. For example, a company might only retain transactions from the past five years or customers located in certain regions. This reduces the dataset to a manageable and meaningful size.

When dealing with semi-structured data, such as JSON logs or API responses, filtering often involves parsing nested fields and removing records that don't match business logic. For instance, an API log might record thousands of "ping" health checks, but the data engineer only needs user-generated actions such as purchases or clicks. Filtering at this level avoids polluting analytics with irrelevant noise.

For unstructured data, filtering is less about strict schemas and more about identifying relevant content. Consider a text corpus scraped from social media. The engineer might filter out retweets, spam messages, or posts that don't meet a language requirement. Similarly, in image datasets, filtering might involve excluding corrupted files or irrelevant formats before the transformation stage continues.

At its core, filtering is about efficiency and relevance. By cutting away what doesn't matter early, pipelines become leaner, costs go down, and the insights derived at the end are sharper.

Deduplication

Another one of the most common issues in raw data is duplication. Duplicates can creep in from multiple sources: repeated extracts from APIs, overlapping datasets from different systems, or human errors such as uploading the same file multiple times. If left unchecked, duplicates can inflate counts, distort metrics, and reduce the reliability of downstream analytics. Deduplication ensures that each record is represented only once in the final dataset.

In relational databases or tabular data, deduplication often involves removing duplicate rows that have identical values across key fields. For example, a customer might appear twice in a CRM export because of a system glitch, with both rows showing the same customer ID. SQL queries using DISTINCT or window functions like ROW_NUMBER() help identify and eliminate these redundant entries. Deduplication in structured datasets usually revolves around defining the correct primary key or unique constraint.

With formats like JSON or XML, duplicates often take the form of repeated nested objects or redundant records collected from APIs. For instance, a JSON log of e-commerce activity might include the same order logged multiple times due to retries or system lag. Data engineers might need to compare unique identifiers inside the JSON (such as order_id or transaction_id) and write scripts that filter out records with repeated IDs.

Deduplication in unstructured contexts can be more nuanced. Consider a dataset of scraped web articles where the same story is copied across multiple websites, or a corpus of images where the same photo appears with different filenames. Here, simple field-based comparisons won't suffice. Instead, data engineers may use hashing techniques to generate checksums for text or image content and then identify duplicates based on those hashes. In some cases, machine learning models are used to detect near-duplicates, such as images with minor changes or slightly reworded text.

Beyond saving storage space, deduplication is about data integrity. Imagine running a revenue forecast where sales orders are accidentally counted twice. Or a churn model that assumes you have twice as many customers leaving because of duplicate entries. Deduplication ensures that downstream analysis reflects reality, not errors in collection.

Standardization

When data is collected from multiple sources, it rarely arrives in a consistent format. Dates may be written as 01/12/2024 in one system and 2024-12-01 in another. Customer names might be entered in different cases like john doe, John Doe, or even DOE, JOHN. Units of measurement may vary as well, with one dataset using miles and another using kilometers. Without standardization, these inconsistencies make it nearly impossible to integrate, query, or analyze data at scale.

In relational databases or tabular formats, standardization often focuses on ensuring consistency across key fields such as dates, numeric values, and identifiers. A classic example is converting all date fields into ISO 8601 (YYYY-MM-DD) format, which prevents misinterpretation across regional formats. Another is ensuring currency values include both amount and currency code (e.g., 100 USD rather than just 100). Standardization here usually involves transformation functions within SQL queries or ETL scripts.

Semi-structured formats like JSON or XML present different challenges because the same type of information may be stored under different keys or in different nested structures. For instance, one JSON file may record a customer's phone number as "phone_number", while another calls it "contactNumber". A data engineer may create mapping logic to unify these into a single field name. Standardization in semi-structured data also involves normalizing inconsistent values like "Yes", "Y", and true into one consistent boolean representation.

Even unstructured data benefits from standardization. Consider scraped text documents where product names appear in inconsistent forms. Standardizing brand names, product IDs, or even spelling variations makes the data much easier to search and analyze. For images or audio, metadata like timestamps, geolocation, or file naming conventions may be standardized so that files can be indexed and organized effectively.

Standardization ensures that data from multiple sources can be combined without creating confusion or errors. Imagine trying to compare sales data when customer IDs are sometimes stored as numbers and sometimes as strings. Standardization removes these ambiguities and allows downstream analytics, business intelligence, and machine learning models to work with consistent, reliable inputs.

Normalization

While standardization ensures that data looks the same across systems, normalization ensures that data is shaped in a way that is efficient, consistent, and useful for analysis. In relational databases, normalization often refers to designing tables in a way that avoids duplication and enforces consistency. This is where database "normal forms" (like 1NF, 2NF, 3NF) come into play. These are guidelines for structuring tables to reduce redundancy and maintain consistency. At a high level, they mean making sure each column holds simple values (1NF), ensuring that every column depends on the whole primary key (2NF), and removing indirect dependencies between non-key columns (3NF). For example, instead of storing a customer's address in every row of a sales table, the address is stored in a separate customer table and referenced by an ID.

For numerical data, normalization may also mean scaling values into a common range, such as converting all test scores into a 0–1 scale or adjusting currencies into a single base currency. This is especially critical in machine learning pipelines, where algorithms can be biased by differences in magnitude between features.

Normalization here often means flattening or restructuring JSON or XML so that it's more usable. For instance, if one dataset records "order_items" as an array inside an order record, a data engineer might normalize it by splitting the array into a separate table where each row corresponds to one item. This allows more precise querying and easier integration with structured systems.

For unstructured sources, normalization often involves converting data into a more regular format. A collection of PDFs might be normalized by extracting text into a tabular format. Image files might be normalized by resizing them to the same dimensions or converting them to a standard color format. Logs from different applications may be normalized into a common schema with fields like timestamp, log level, and message.

Normalization improves both performance and reliability. Without it, systems can end up storing duplicate information, creating unnecessary storage costs and increasing the risk of inconsistencies. In analytics and machine learning, unnormalized data can produce misleading results, since values are comparable. By carefully normalizing, data engineers ensure that downstream processes can interpret and process the data correctly, whether it's a simple business intelligence dashboard or a predictive model.

Data Quality Verification

Accuracy and completeness are two of the most important dimensions of data quality, and both need to be checked during the Transform step. Accuracy means validating that the data reflects reality. For structured sources like relational databases, this might involve checking whether all foreign keys match valid primary keys or whether numeric fields fall within expected ranges.

For semi-structured or unstructured sources, accuracy checks could include verifying that JSON fields are present and valid or that log files contain complete timestamps. These rules are often implemented directly in the pipeline or automated as part of testing frameworks to confirm the integrity of every incoming batch.

Completeness ensures that nothing critical is missing. If a sales table is missing an entire day's worth of transactions, dashboards and forecasts will be misleading. Completeness checks might include row counts, comparing expected totals with actuals, or scanning for null values in mandatory fields. Some organizations also use "control totals," pre-calculated aggregates that act as quick reference points to confirm that datasets are fully loaded.

To operationalize these checks, many organizations embed automated data quality verification directly into their pipelines. Tools like Great Expectations, data build tool (dbt) tests, or custom Python and PySpark scripts can enforce constraints, flag issues, and trigger alerts if thresholds are violated. Results are logged so that the history of data quality is trackable over time, making root cause analysis easier when problems arise.

Placing verification and accuracy checks in the Transform step is critical because this is where data is shaped and prepared for downstream use. If issues are detected here, they can often be corrected through the techniques discussed above before the data reaches a warehouse or analytics system. Without verification at this stage, bad data may slip through unchanged, becoming harder and more expensive to fix later.

Transforming Between Data Types

A data engineer's work often centers on reshaping data so it can be stored, queried, and analyzed effectively. One common task is turning unstructured information into structured form. Customer feedback in free text can be distilled into themes or ratings, and server logs can be parsed into fields such as timestamp, address, and response time. These steps convert raw, messy inputs into data that systems can interpret and act on.

Semi-structured data also carries useful signals but often needs to be flattened or reorganized. A nested product catalog may need to be normalized into a tabular format before it can be joined with sales records. The aim is to impose enough order on flexible structures to support consistent queries, joins, and downstream analytics.

Structured data sometimes must be reshaped to match different conventions or levels of detail. A system that stores numeric category codes may need to align with another that expects descriptive labels, and detailed transactions may need to be rolled up into weekly or quarterly summaries. In each case, the goal is compatibility and comparability across systems and use cases.

Data Enrichment

Data enrichment is the process of enhancing existing data by adding new information, either from internal systems or external sources, to provide additional context, accuracy, and value. While extraction brings in raw data and transformation standardizes and validates it, enrichment makes the data more useful for decision-making by filling in gaps or connecting it to broader datasets.

Many enrichment activities draw on data already within an organization. For example, a transaction dataset may include customer IDs but not demographic details. A data engineer can enrich the transaction data by joining it with a customer master table to add attributes such as age, location, or account type. Similarly, enriching log files with application metadata, such as error codes or server regions, helps teams trace issues more effectively.

Sometimes, the most valuable context comes from outside the organization. For instance, enriching addresses in a customer database with geospatial data enables location-based analytics. An e-commerce platform might add weather data to sales records to understand how climate influences purchasing behavior, or financial firms may enhance market transaction data with news feeds and sentiment analysis. External APIs and third-party data providers are common tools for these tasks, with engineers responsible for integrating them in a scalable and compliant way.

Let's take a look at some examples of data enrichment in practice. A retail company, for instance, may combine census data with sales records to analyze customer behavior by region and socioeconomic status. A logistics firm might enrich shipment tracking data with traffic and weather feeds in order to improve delivery time estimates. Similarly, a SaaS platform can augment user activity logs with device and browser details to better understand usage patterns and guide product design decisions.

Data enrichment often relies on joins, lookups, and API calls. At scale, tools like Apache Spark or dbt can be used to automate the integration of large datasets, while cloud services such as AWS Data Exchange or Google's BigQuery public datasets provide ready-made enrichment sources. The challenge lies in ensuring data consistency and avoiding over-enrichment, where unnecessary details make the dataset too large or cumbersome.

Without enrichment, data often tells only part of the story. By layering additional information onto core datasets, data engineers help organizations make more informed, nuanced decisions. Enriched data powers better customer segmentation, more accurate predictive models, and clearer insights across departments.

Common Pitfalls in the Transformation Stage

A frequent challenge in the Transform stage is data loss or over-transformation. When values are rounded too early, data is aggregated at the wrong level, or outliers are discarded without proper analysis, important context disappears. Once this detail is stripped away, datasets become less flexible for future use cases, often locking them into a single narrow application.

Another recurring issue is inconsistency across pipelines. If different teams define their own rules for cleaning and standardizing, the results can be fragmented. One job may encode missing values as NULL, another as -999, and a third as an empty string. These differences make downstream reconciliation messy and can undermine confidence in analytics. At the same time, poorly optimized transformations create performance bottlenecks. Joins that are not written efficiently, Python scripts that are not vectorized, or jobs that fail to parallelize can all slow the system and drive up costs.

Transformation also carries compliance and privacy risks. Joining or enriching datasets can inadvertently expose sensitive information, even re-identifying individuals thought to be anonymized. Without proper masking or tokenization, privacy laws such as GDPR or HIPAA can be violated. A column name change or type modification in a source database can silently break transformations, producing corrupted or partial outputs. Finally, a lack of documentation and transparency turns pipelines into "black boxes." Analysts may not understand what manipulations have been applied, and small mistakes in transformation logic can ripple downstream, propagating errors across reports, dashboards, and models.

Best Practices for the Transformation Stage

To counter these risks, data engineers follow a set of practices that preserve quality, efficiency, and trust. First, always keep an untouched copy of raw data in a staging area or data lake. This safeguard allows teams to revisit the original source if a mistake is uncovered or if new use cases require detail that was previously aggregated away. Transformation rules should also be standardized across teams. Shared conventions for null handling, date and time formats, and currency conversions ensure that outputs from different pipelines remain consistent and interoperable.

Validation is most effective when applied continuously rather than at the end. Checks for schema alignment before transformations, outlier detection after aggregations, and logging of unexpected values help catch issues before they spread. Equally important is designing for scale. Use vectorized operations, distributed frameworks like Apache Spark, or push transformations into the database where appropriate. Queries should be tested on production-sized datasets to confirm they perform efficiently.

Respecting privacy must be embedded in every step. Sensitive identifiers should be anonymized or masked as early as possible, and no external enrichment should be attempted without explicit compliance review. Because schema drift is inevitable, automate schema checks that detect changes in field names, types, or expected values. Quick alerts prevent silent breakages from corrupting downstream data.

Transparency is another pillar of best practice. Document why fields were dropped, how outliers were treated, and which enrichment sources were chosen. Pair documentation with metadata and lineage tracking so that consumers understand both the logic and provenance of the data. Finally, treat transformation logic as production code. Unit tests, integration tests, and regression tests should confirm correctness and prevent accidental changes from slipping into production.

Together, these practices make the transformation stage resilient. They guard against the loss of valuable context, ensure compliance, and deliver outputs that users can trust.

Load

The final step of the ETL pipeline is the Load stage, where data that has been extracted and transformed is delivered into its destination system. This could be a data warehouse, a data lake, an operational database, or even a downstream application that depends on fresh data. While extraction is about getting the right data out of its source, and transformation is about shaping it into the correct format, loading is about making sure that data arrives in the target environment safely, accurately, and efficiently.

Loading might sound straightforward, like simply writing the data into a table or system but in practice, it's also a complicated part of the pipeline. Poorly designed loading processes can overwhelm a target system, introduce latency, or even corrupt the final dataset. Because this is the stage where data becomes available for use by analysts, business intelligence tools, or machine learning models, it's also the stage most directly tied to the reliability and trustworthiness of the entire pipeline.

In modern data engineering, there are several approaches to loading data. Some pipelines rely on batch loads, where large chunks of data are delivered at once on a schedule. Others use streaming loads, which deliver records in near real time. The choice depends on business needs: a financial application may require second-by-second updates, while a retail dashboard might only need nightly refreshes. Beyond timing, engineers must also decide whether to use full loads where data is replaced entirely, or incremental loads, where only changes since the last load are applied. Each option comes with trade-offs in performance, cost, and complexity.

The Load stage is where the hard work of ETL becomes visible to the organization. A successful loading process ensures that the cleaned, transformed data flows into the right place at the right time, powering decision-making with confidence. In the sections that follow, we'll explore the different strategies for loading data, the challenges that can arise, and the best practices that can help data engineers design pipelines that are both resilient and efficient.

Batch Jobs

Batch jobs are one of the oldest and most widely used strategies for delivering data into a target system. In this approach, data is collected during a period of time, grouped into a batch, and then loaded into the destination all at once. This is common in organizations where business processes operate on a daily or hourly cadence, such as updating sales figures overnight or refreshing dashboards at the start of each workday.

The advantage of batch jobs is their inherent simplicity. By handling data in chunks, engineers can design repeatable jobs that run at predictable times. This reduces complexity compared to constantly streaming small updates and allows the organization to plan around regular refresh windows. Batch processes are also easier to debug since all the data for a given run is collected in one place and failures can often be retried without impacting upstream systems.

However, batch jobs come with trade-offs. If a process fails, large volumes of data may be delayed, leaving dashboards or analytics stale until the issue is resolved. Because batch jobs often run at peak business hours or overnight, they can put stress on systems, particularly if not tuned correctly. Finally, batch approaches are not well-suited to use cases that require real-time or near real-time data, such as fraud detection or live customer personalization.

Despite these challenges, batch jobs remain a core strategy in data engineering. Many organizations pair it with downstream tools to orchestrate the runs and ensure data arrives in the right format at the right time. It continues to be an excellent fit for predictable, repeatable workflows where real-time updates aren't mission critical.

Streaming Jobs

We explored streaming architectures in the extract section, but it's worth noting their role again here in the context of loading. Streaming jobs are designed for scenarios where data must be delivered into the target system in real time or near real time. Instead of waiting for a batch process to run, data is ingested continuously as it's generated. This enables use cases such as live dashboards tracking customer behavior, fraud detection systems that respond within seconds, or recommendation engines that update instantly as users interact with a platform.

The main advantage of streaming is timeliness: decisions can be made using the most current information available. However, this comes with trade-offs. Streaming systems are typically more complex to design and operate, and they require thoughtful approaches to handling issues like duplicate records, delayed events, and continuous quality checks. They may also incur higher costs, since the infrastructure needs to be "always on."

Hybrid Jobs (Batch + Streaming)

Many organizations find that neither pure batch nor pure streaming loads meet all their needs. Hybrid jobs combine both approaches so data can be delivered quickly without sacrificing long-term accuracy or cost efficiency. In a hybrid design, the streaming layer delivers provisional records to downstream systems in near real time, while the batch layer refreshes and reconciles those same records on a scheduled cadence.

A common pattern is to land events in a streaming store so they are immediately available for dashboards, personalization, or alerts, and then run a nightly or hourly batch load that replaces or upserts the same period with authoritative results. In this model, the streaming path keeps operational systems fresh, while the batch path ensures that late-arriving events, reordered records, and other discrepancies are resolved before data is considered final.

Designing a hybrid load requires clear handoffs. Teams must decide which outputs from the streaming layer are provisional and which outputs from the batch layer are authoritative. Consistent keys and time windows make it possible for the batch load to overwrite or reconcile earlier streaming loads. Partitioning data by event time or ingestion time further simplifies replay and backfill. Documenting these handoffs ensures that stakeholders understand when numbers may change and when they can be trusted as final.

Cost and reliability also benefit from this approach. By keeping the streaming load lean—focused only on what must be delivered immediately—organizations can reduce system overhead. Heavy operations can be deferred to batch loads that run during off-peak hours, when resources are cheaper and more predictable. Monitoring that compares streaming and batch counts for the same time windows helps detect gaps or inconsistencies, ensuring that both layers stay aligned.

Over time, hybrid jobs can be tuned by adjusting batch frequency and streaming window sizes, striking the right balance between immediacy and accuracy for the business.

Up to this point, we've focused on strategies that determine when data is moved, referring to the batch, streaming, and hybrid approaches. Equally important, however, are the strategies that determine how data is written once it reaches the target. Two of the most common methods are full loading and incremental loading, each with its own trade-offs in terms of efficiency, complexity, and reliability.

Full Loading

Full loading is the simplest loading strategy. Every time the pipeline runs, it replaces the contents of the target table or dataset with the latest version of the source. This guarantees that the destination is fully in sync with the source and avoids the risk of missing updates. However, it can be expensive and inefficient because the system has to process all records, even if only a few changes. Full loads can put pressure on network bandwidth, storage, and compute, so they are usually only practical for small datasets or for cases where the business needs a guaranteed fresh snapshot.

Imagine a retail company that maintains a reference table of product categories: Electronics, Clothing, Home Goods, and so on. The table might only contain a few hundred rows, updated infrequently when new categories are introduced or old ones are retired. Instead of designing incremental logic to detect whether "Outdoor Equipment" was added or whether "Video Games" was renamed, the pipeline simply reloads the entire table every night. This guarantees that analysts working on sales dashboards always have the most current category definitions, while keeping the pipeline simple, transparent, and easy to maintain. In this case, the small size and stability of the dataset make full loading the most practical choice.

Incremental Loading

Incremental loading only moves new or changed data since the last pipeline run. Instead of replacing the entire dataset, it appends or updates records in the destination. This is far more efficient for large, frequently changing tables because it minimizes data transfer and processing. Incremental loads rely on mechanisms to detect changes, such as timestamps, version numbers, or CDC.

When we discussed extraction, we looked at CDC as a way to consume changes from a source system — essentially listening to database logs to see what has been inserted, updated, or deleted. In the load phase, CDC plays the opposite role. Here, the pipeline becomes the producer of change events, applying those same inserts, updates, and deletes into the destination system. Instead of bulk overwriting tables, the load process replays changes incrementally, keeping the warehouse or lake in sync with the source.

For example, if a sales record was updated at the source, the load step issues the corresponding update in the warehouse rather than reloading all sales data. This approach is more efficient, preserves history when needed, and reduces compute and storage costs. Here, CDC ensures the destination system reflects the source system's state as faithfully and efficiently as possible [52].

Schema Evolution and Compatibility

One of the most overlooked challenges in the Load stage is dealing with change. Business requirements shift, new features roll out, and suddenly the schema of your source or target system isn't the same as yesterday. If a pipeline blindly loads data without accounting for these changes, it risks failing outright or, worse, silently corrupting the dataset.

Schema evolution refers to the ability of a pipeline and target system to adapt as fields are added, removed, or modified. For example, a customer table might introduce a new loyalty_status column, or an order_total field might change from INT to DECIMAL. Without proper safeguards, loads could reject the data or misinterpret values.

To handle these challenges, data engineers often rely on schema management strategies. One common approach is schema validation, where incoming data is checked against the expected structure before a load is committed. When new fields appear, default values and null handling can provide sensible fallbacks so downstream queries don't break. Some teams use versioning, maintaining multiple versions of a table or view so consumers can transition gradually. In event-driven systems, schema registries help enforce consistency by ensuring that producers and consumers agree on field names and data types. Together, these practices help pipelines remain stable even as schemas evolve.

Compatibility is key. Forward compatibility ensures new data can still be read by old consumers; backward compatibility ensures old data can still be read after a schema change. When designing a load process, it's best to plan for both so pipelines remain resilient as the business evolves.

Tools and Technologies for Loading

The core loading strategies–batch versus streaming and full versus incremental–are universal, but their implementation depends heavily on the tools you choose. Modern data engineering offers no shortage of options: some are built directly into cloud warehouses, others come as managed services, specialized open-source frameworks, or even custom software you write yourself. Navigating this landscape is essential, as the right choice determines how well a pipeline balances performance, reliability, cost, and long-term maintainability.

Cloud data warehouses such as Snowflake, BigQuery, and Amazon Redshift provide built-in commands for fast, parallelized data loading. For example, Snowflake's COPY INTO command can bulk-load data directly from Amazon S3, Azure Blob Storage, or Google Cloud Storage [53]. These loaders handle partitioning and compression automatically, making them highly efficient for large-scale batch operations. Similarly, Redshift's COPY command can ingest terabytes of data in parallel from S3, DynamoDB, or EMR clusters [54]. BigQuery supports both batch loads (bq load) and streaming inserts, giving flexibility for organizations that need a mix of historical backfills and real-time updates.

The benefit of warehouse-native loaders is speed and tight integration. Since they're built into the target platform, they take advantage of columnar storage formats, optimized file ingestion, and native parallelism. However, they generally require the data to already be staged in cloud object storage, so an upstream process is often needed to get files into the right format and location.

Sometimes, business needs go beyond what commercial or managed tools offer. In those cases, open-source frameworks and custom loaders provide maximum flexibility. Apache Spark Structured Streaming and Apache Flink are popular for handling high-throughput, low-latency streaming loads. They can ingest millions of events per second, transform the data in real time, and deliver it into warehouses, databases, or even machine learning feature stores.

For more tailored solutions, engineers often write custom loaders in Python, Java, or Scala, leveraging libraries like SQLAlchemy, psycopg2, or JDBC drivers. Custom loaders allow for fine-grained control over batch sizes, parallelism, retries, and error handling, as well as support for niche systems that may not have off-the-shelf connectors. While they require more engineering effort to build and maintain, they can provide unmatched flexibility and performance tuning.

Loading Approaches by Destination

The choice of destination system has a huge impact on how data engineers design the Load stage. Each type of target, whether it's a data lake, an operational database, or an application comes with its own expectations for performance, latency, schema handling, and cost. A well-designed load strategy aligns not just with the volume of data but also with how that data will be consumed downstream.

When the target is a data lake (e.g., Amazon S3, Azure Data Lake, Google Cloud Storage), the emphasis shifts to raw, flexible storage. Data lakes are schema-on-read, meaning engineers often dump files in formats like Parquet, ORC, or Avro without enforcing rigid schemas at load time. Loads here are less about SQL efficiency and more about durability, partitioning, and cost. Partitioning by time or event type makes future queries faster, while formats like Parquet compress well and keep compute costs down. Data lakes are often paired with warehouse layers (like Snowflake or Databricks) that query the data later with more structure.

Operational databases (PostgreSQL, MySQL, MongoDB) serve live applications and transactional workloads. Here, load jobs must be much more careful: bulk operations can lock tables and impact performance for end users. Instead, engineers may design incremental upserts (insert + update) using batching to reduce contention. They might throttle loads during off-peak hours or replicate data asynchronously using CDC pipelines. Reliability and minimal impact on application latency take priority over sheer throughput.

Some destinations are not databases at all, but business-facing applications like Salesforce, HubSpot, or BI platforms like Tableau and Power BI. These systems usually have strict APIs and rate limits, so data engineers rely on connectors (like Fivetran or custom-built loaders) that respect quotas and handle retries gracefully. Loading strategies here prioritize accuracy, freshness, and compliance—it's better to have slightly stale CRM data than to overload an API and lose synchronization entirely.

For streaming use cases—fraud detection, personalization, IoT telemetry—the target may be a streaming store or feature store, such as Kafka topics, Kinesis streams, or Redis. Engineers design pipelines that push events continuously, often with exactly-once or at-least-once delivery guarantees. These destinations care about low latency and consistency rather than bulk throughput. In practice, many organizations pair these real-time loads with batch reconciliation into a warehouse or lake to keep the official records consistent.

Common Pitfalls in the Load Stage

Although loading data may sound like the simplest part of the pipeline, it's often where things go wrong. Because this is the stage where data becomes available to the rest of the organization, errors here can have the most visible and damaging impact.

One common pitfall is overloading the destination system. A poorly tuned batch job that tries to push millions of rows at once can overwhelm a database, causing query slowdowns or even outages for other users. Similarly, a streaming pipeline without backpressure controls can flood a warehouse with duplicate or incomplete records.

Another issue is lack of idempotency, that is, the ability to safely re-run a load without duplicating or corrupting data. If a job fails halfway and simply starts again without safeguards, the warehouse may end up with duplicate rows or missing updates. Without careful design, retries can make problems worse instead of fixing them.

Finally, there is the pitfall of loading without validation. It's tempting to assume that if the data has already been extracted and transformed, it can be safely loaded. But failures in earlier stages or subtle issues like out-of-order timestamps or missing keys can still surface here. A source system might add a new column, change a datatype, or drop a field without notice, breaking the load step entirely. If the load process doesn't include sanity checks, the target may silently accumulate bad data that erodes trust over time.

Best Practices for the Load Stage

The good news is that with careful planning, these pitfalls can be avoided. Successful load strategies emphasize safety, efficiency, and reliability.

A first best practice is to design loads to be idempotent. This means that if a job is re-run, the outcome is the same as if it ran only once. In practice, this often means using MERGE or UPSERT logic in SQL warehouses instead of blind inserts, or partitioning loads by date so that re-processing a partition cleanly replaces the old data.

Another key practice is monitoring and validation. Always compare source and destination row counts, check for nulls in required fields, and verify data freshness. Many teams build automated data quality checks into the load step so that errors are caught immediately rather than weeks later when a business user notices a report looks wrong.

Schema evolution management is equally important. Instead of letting schema drift break jobs, build in compatibility checks and default handling. For example, if a new column appears, it can be automatically set to NULL until downstream transformations are updated. Schema registries and versioning strategies are also powerful tools for keeping track of changes.

On the performance side, it's best to leverage warehouse-native bulk loading commands rather than row-by-row inserts. Partitioning and clustering large tables, staging files in object storage, and compressing data before load all make the process faster and cheaper. For streaming systems, implement rate limiting and backpressure to avoid overwhelming the destination.

Lastly, document and communicate service-level expectations around the load stage. Stakeholders should know when data will be fresh (e.g., "sales data is loaded every night by 6 AM") and when metrics are provisional (e.g., "real-time dashboard data may differ from nightly batch reports"). Setting clear expectations builds trust and prevents confusion when numbers don't align.

ETL vs. ELT

When people talk about data pipelines today, two acronyms dominate the conversation: ETL (Extract, Transform, Load) and ELT (Extract, Load, Transform). At first glance, the difference seems small—just a minute order change of the letters—but in practice these two approaches reflect very different design philosophies and historical contexts in data engineering. Understanding both is important to make thoughtful choices about how to build pipelines that serve business needs.

ETL is the traditional model. Data is first extracted from source systems, then transformed into a clean, structured format, and finally loaded into the target database or warehouse. This approach emerged in the era when warehouses were costly and limited in both compute and storage. It made sense to do as much of the heavy lifting as possible outside of the warehouse, ensuring that only curated, ready-to-use data entered the final system. ETL has the advantage of strict control: transformations are applied before the data ever touches the warehouse, which helps with governance, compliance, and ensuring that downstream users work only with vetted datasets.

ELT, by contrast, is a newer approach that became popular with the rising adoption of cloud data warehouses over traditional. Instead of transforming data first, ELT pipelines load raw or lightly processed data directly into the warehouse, and then perform transformations inside the target system. The logic here is simple: modern warehouses are fast, elastic, and cheap compared to older systems, so why not take advantage of their compute power to do the work? This approach gives analysts more flexibility, since raw data is available for exploration, and transformations can be written directly in SQL or orchestrated with tools like dbt.

Neither approach is inherently better and ultimately it comes down to trade-offs. ETL pipelines enforce discipline and prevent warehouses from becoming cluttered with raw, messy, or sensitive data. They are especially useful in industries with strict compliance requirements like those related to financials or healthcare, or in cases where the business wants a single, highly curated version of the truth. ELT pipelines, on the other hand, excel in speed and agility. Raw data lands quickly, giving teams immediate access, and transformations can evolve iteratively as new business questions arise. The trade-off is that warehouses can become sprawling and harder to govern if transformations are well managed.

For this book, we mostly focus on ETL. The reason is that ETL offers a clear, structured way to introduce the concepts of data pipelines: how data is extracted, how it's transformed into usable formats, and how it's loaded into destination systems. It's also the model that forces engineers to think carefully about data quality, schema design, and governance, concepts that remain foundational no matter which approach you ultimately use. That said, it would be incomplete to ignore ELT. Many organizations today rely heavily on ELT, especially those that have invested in cloud warehouses. Being aware of both models and knowing when to apply one or the other is part of the craft.

In practice, the line between ETL and ELT is often blurred. A pipeline may filter or validate some data before loading it (an ETL-like step), then perform heavy joins and aggregations in the warehouse (an ELT-like step). The decision is rarely absolute, and often depends on the strengths of the tools at hand, the nature of the data, and the expectations of the business. Whether you lean toward ETL or ELT, the underlying goal is the same: to deliver data that is accurate, reliable, and available in the right form at the right time.

Examples: ETL vs. ELT

To make the distinction clearer, it helps to look at how ETL and ELT are applied in different industries. Your choice will depend on technology, business priorities, compliance requirements, and the kinds of decisions organizations need to make from their data.

Hospitals and research institutions deal with highly sensitive patient information, often subject to strict regulations like HIPAA in the United States. In this environment, an ETL pipeline makes more sense. Before data ever enters a centralized system, transformations can be applied to mask personally identifiable information, standardize medical codes, and validate that only clean, compliant records are retained. By the time the data is loaded into a warehouse, it's already curated and safe for use by doctors, researchers, or administrators. The focus here is governance and trustworthiness: every field must be correct, every record must comply with regulation, and there is little room for ambiguity.

Now consider e-commerce. Online retailers generate enormous amounts of semi-structured data in the form of clickstreams, shopping cart updates, inventory feeds, and payment transactions. Speed is critical, since customer behavior can change minute by minute. For these organizations, ELT often provides the best fit. Raw event data can be loaded directly into a cloud warehouse where transformations can be applied on demand. Analysts might build models to understand abandoned carts, product recommendations, or fraud detection, and they need the flexibility to iterate quickly. Having raw data available in the warehouse means they can test new ideas without waiting for upstream pipeline changes. Here, the priority is agility and responsiveness, even if it means the warehouse holds messier, less-governed datasets alongside the polished ones.

Chapter 5
Data Needs a Story

"The goal is to turn data into information,
and information into insight."

– Carly Fiorina [55]

Business Intelligence

Business Intelligence (BI) is the practice of turning raw data into meaningful insights that guide decision-making. It combines data collection, cleaning, and analysis with tools to create dashboards, reports, and visualizations. Business intelligence aims to make complex data understandable and actionable for businesses. While data engineers aren't usually responsible for building dashboards or presenting polished visual reports, their work is the backbone that makes modern business intelligence platforms possible. These platforms like Tableau, Microsoft Power BI, Looker, and Qlik, sit at the final stage of the data pipeline, where stakeholders and decision-makers interact with data in a way that's accessible and actionable. As you already know, a data engineer's role is to make sure the data that feeds into these systems is accurate, reliable, and timely.

By knowing the expectations of BI tools, a data engineer can build pipelines that have the ability to deliver data in a format that downstream users can immediately leverage. For example, analysts working in Tableau may expect data to arrive in a star schema that supports fast slicing and filtering [56]. Power BI users may lean on DirectQuery or import modes that change how queries hit the warehouse [57]. Looker relies heavily on its semantic layer, which means engineers need to deliver clean, well-labeled tables for modeling [58].

These platforms also highlight a key truth in data engineering: data is only valuable if it's usable. Even the most advanced data pipeline holds little business value if the data is locked away in complex schemas or raw logs. Business intelligence bridges this gap by enabling non-technical stakeholders to explore trends, measure performance, and make decisions. For this reason, while data engineers may never drag and drop a chart inside Tableau, they should still understand the role these tools play, and how their work feeds directly into them.

Tableau

Tableau has long been one of the most widely used business intelligence platforms, prized for its ability to turn raw datasets into highly visual dashboards with little technical overhead for the end user. Its drag-and-drop interface allows analysts, managers, and even executives to explore data without needing to write SQL or code. From a data engineering standpoint, however, Tableau's ease of use for the front end often creates challenges on the back end.

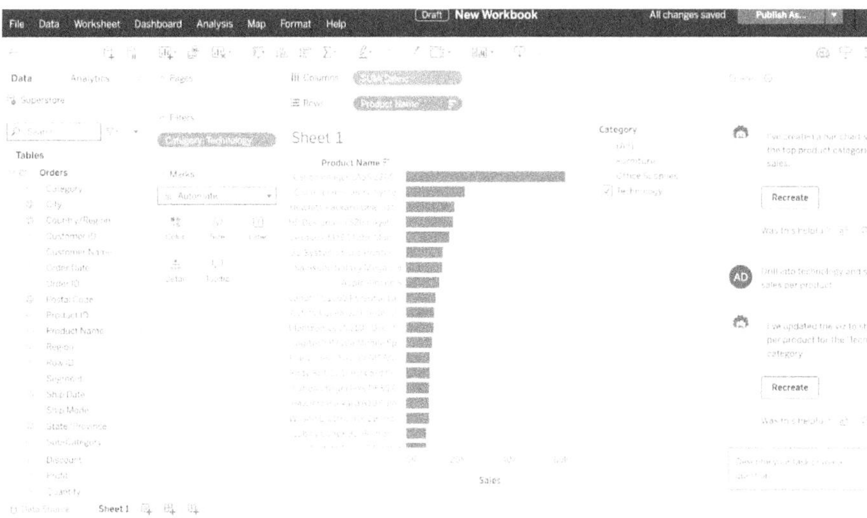

Figure 10: A Tableau UI [59]

Tableau works best when it's supplied with data that's already been modeled for analysis. If engineers provide raw transactional tables, dashboards can become slow, confusing, or even misleading. For example, attempting to calculate revenue from an unstructured set of order and refund logs could result in duplicate counts, null values, or overly complex calculations. To avoid this, engineers often prepare star or snowflake schemas that Tableau can query efficiently, ensuring that metrics are clean, consistent, and fast to compute [60].

Another important consideration with Tableau is data extracts. When datasets are very large, Tableau can cache portions of

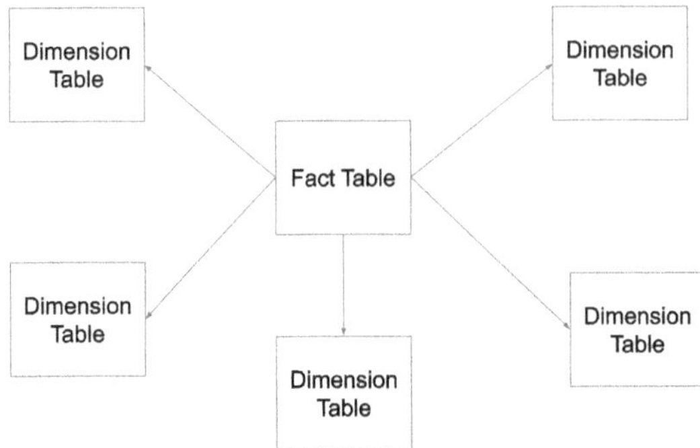

Figure 11: A General Star Schema

the data into extracts to improve performance. Engineers may be asked to schedule or manage these extracts so that dashboards update at regular intervals without overwhelming the source systems. Additionally, because Tableau users often create their own custom dashboards, engineers may find themselves responsible for building centralized, trusted data sources so that "Revenue" or "Customer Count" always means the same thing across the organization. In many enterprises, Tableau becomes the face of the data stack, which means the quality of the upstream pipelines is directly reflected in the trust users place in the dashboards.

Microsoft Power BI

Microsoft Power BI has quickly become one of the fastest growing BI platforms, especially among organizations that are already invested in the Microsoft ecosystem. It integrates naturally with Azure, SQL Server, and even Excel, which lowers the barrier to adoption for businesses that already rely on those tools. From the perspective of a data engineer, Power BI introduces some unique opportunities and constraints that shape how pipelines are built.

Power BI offers two main modes of connecting to data: Import and DirectQuery. In Import mode, data is pulled into Power BI's in-memory engine, which makes dashboards lightning-fast but requires thoughtful management of refresh schedules. In Di-

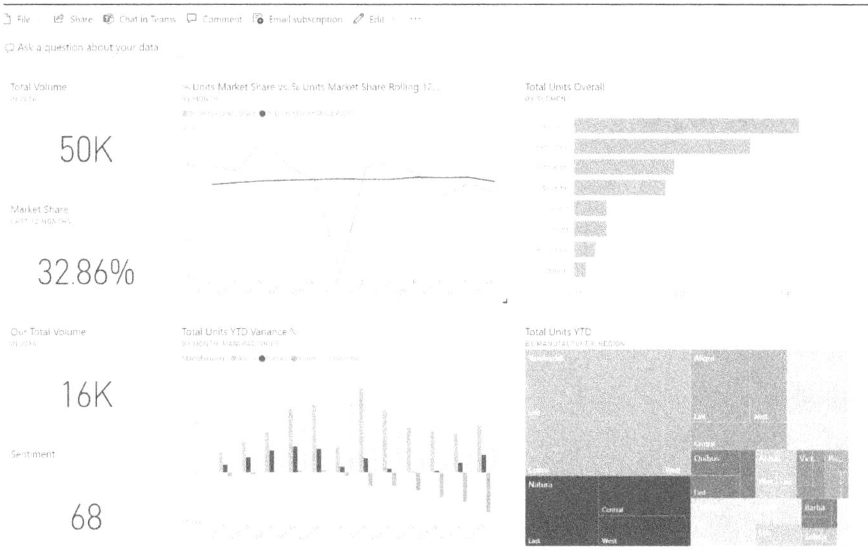

Figure 12: A Microsoft Power BI UI [61]

rectQuery mode, queries are executed directly against the source database, which ensures the freshest possible data but places significant stress on the underlying warehouse. This means deciding whether to optimize tables for fast querying (supporting DirectQuery) or for compact snapshots that can be imported and refreshed efficiently [62].

Another notable strength of Power BI is its ability to integrate with Excel, which remains one of the most familiar analysis tools for many business users. Engineers may be tasked with designing data models that allow analysts to move seamlessly between Excel and Power BI dashboards without creating mismatched numbers or duplicate work [63]. Power BI also supports strong role-based access controls, which ties directly into governance considerations [64]. For instance, you may need to partition data so that a regional manager only sees their market's sales data, while executives can view the global roll-up.

Because Power BI is tightly integrated into Microsoft's cloud ecosystem, it's also often used in conjunction with Azure Data Lake and Synapse Analytics. This makes it particularly attractive for organizations building modern, cloud-native warehouses. Understanding how Power BI connects to those systems ensures that pipelines feed into dashboards without bottlenecks.

Google Looker

Looker takes a very different approach compared to Tableau and Power BI. Rather than focusing only on the visualization layer, it introduces a semantic modeling layer called LookML. With LookML, engineers or analytics engineers define dimensions, metrics, and relationships in code [65]. This creates a single version of truth across the organization. For example, once "Gross Revenue" is defined in LookML, every dashboard, report, or ad hoc query that references it will calculate the value in the exact same way.

From a data engineering perspective, this means that Looker is not just a consumer of data, but also an extension of the modeling process. Engineers are often involved in structuring upstream tables so they can be easily modeled in LookML. Clean naming conventions, well-defined joins, and clear primary keys all play a critical

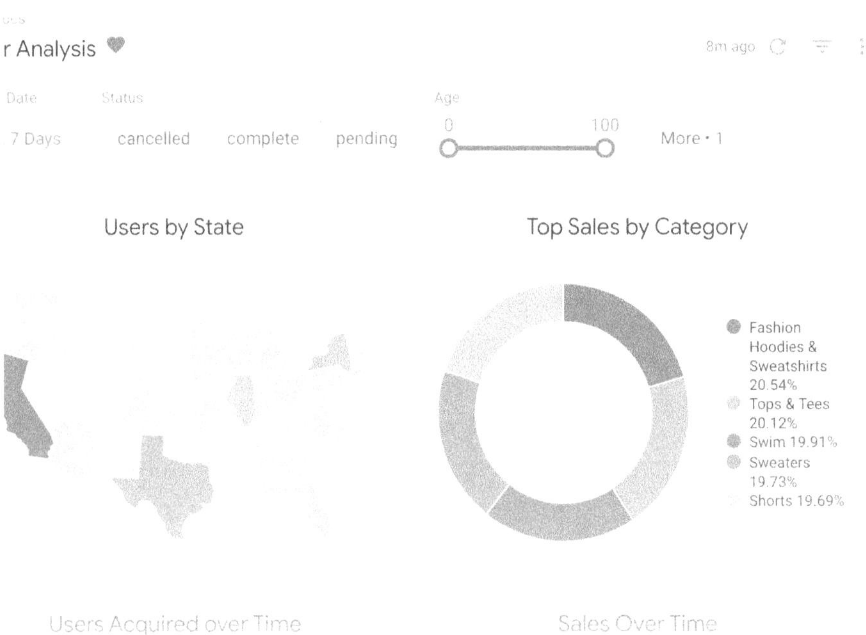

Figure 13: A Google Looker UI [66]

role in making Looker effective. Without these, the semantic layer becomes fragile and confusing.

Another major benefit of Looker is its governance. By centralizing definitions in LookML, it prevents the "Excel sprawl" problem where different teams calculate the same metric differently [67]. It also enables version control, allowing teams to treat their business definitions as code. For engineers, this bridges the gap between the technical data pipelines and the business-facing analytics, creating a smoother collaboration with analysts.

Looker is especially popular among organizations that want strict consistency across reporting. For instance, a fintech company might define regulatory reporting metrics once in LookML, ensuring that compliance reports and executive dashboards never drift out of alignment. While Looker requires more upfront engineering investment than drag-and-drop tools, the payoff is long-term trust and clarity in the organization's data.

Application-Native Dashboards

Enterprise systems such as Salesforce, Workday, ServiceNow, and HubSpot all include reporting layers. For example, Salesforce offers "Reports" and "Dashboards" that allow sales teams to slice pipeline data, measure quota attainment, or monitor activity without ever leaving the CRM [68]. These built-in tools are highly convenient for end-users because they work directly on top of the application's transactional data and require minimal setup. Similar reporting features exist in HR platforms for tracking headcount and turnover, or in marketing automation systems like Adobe's Marketo for campaign performance.

From a data engineer's perspective, application-native dashboards are a double-edged sword. On the one hand, they reduce the need for constant pipeline work since the data is already in the application and refreshed in real time. On the other hand, these tools are usually siloed: a Salesforce dashboard cannot easily incorporate marketing spend from Google Ads or product usage logs from a data warehouse. This fragmentation can create "islands of reporting" where different teams trust different numbers.

Integration With BI Platforms

This is where data engineers add value. Through a thorough ETL/ ELT process, engineers ensure that Salesforce data can be combined with financial data, support tickets, or web analytics. Once centralized, BI platforms like Tableau, Power BI, or Looker can provide a unified, enterprise-wide view. The application dashboards remain useful for day-to-day operational insights, while the BI platforms provide strategic, cross-functional analytics.

Just as business intelligence platforms consume and display data prepared by data engineers, customer relationship management systems like Salesforce, HubSpot, or Microsoft Dynamics depend on a steady flow of accurate and timely data to function effectively. While data engineers are not usually the ones logging into these systems to manage leads or run sales campaigns, they are often the people behind the scenes making sure the data that flows into them is clean, complete, and reliable.

CRM Systems

Customer Relationship Management (CRM) systems serve as the central hub for sales, marketing, and customer service activities. They track everything from customer contact details and purchase histories to sales pipelines and support interactions. For these platforms to be useful, the data that populates them needs to be correct and consistent. That is where the data engineer comes in. By building pipelines that extract customer data from e-commerce platforms, marketing systems, support tools, or even raw transaction logs, engineers ensure that CRMs stay up to date with the latest information.

Knowing how CRMs are structured and what kinds of data they require is valuable even if you aren't working inside the platform daily. Understanding the types of objects Salesforce uses, or how HubSpot organizes marketing and sales workflows, helps you anticipate the data requirements for each department. It also helps

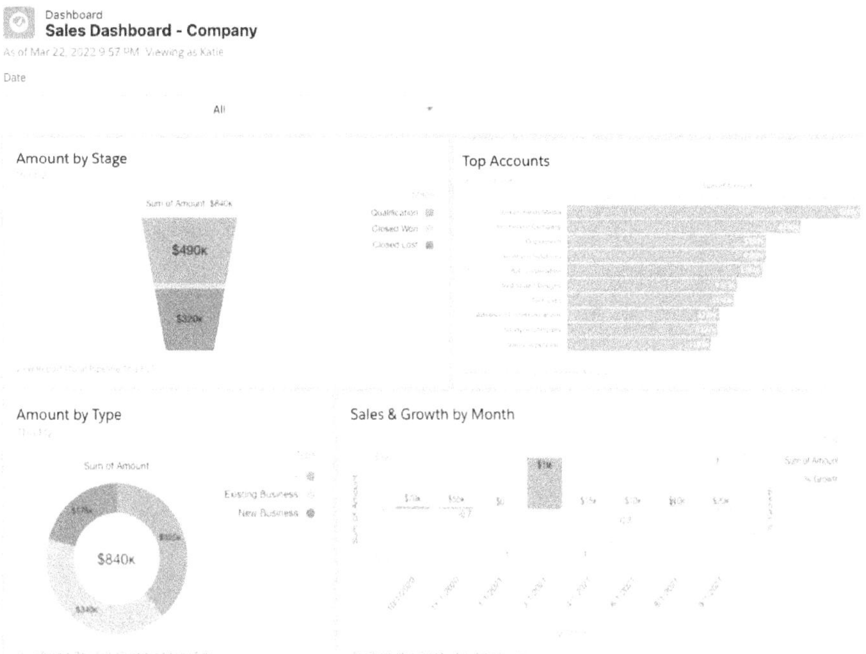

Figure 14: A Salesforce UI [66]

you design ETL processes that enrich these systems with external data, such as customer demographics, web activity, or support histories.

While Salesforce is the most recognized CRM on the market, it's far from the only platform a data engineer might encounter. Each major CRM platform has its own structure and terminology, but they all share the same fundamental need, that being a steady stream of accurate, up-to-date data to support sales, marketing, and customer service teams.

Salesforce is known for its extensive customization and ecosystem of integrations. Data engineers often support Salesforce by supplying data to objects like Accounts, Contacts, Leads, and Opportunities. Many organizations rely on Salesforce's APIs to sync data from their warehouses or third-party tools, and engineers are often the ones writing and maintaining those integrations [70].

HubSpot is another widely used CRM, especially among small and medium-sized businesses. It focuses on marketing automation and inbound sales, and its data model is somewhat simpler than Salesforce. Engineers may be tasked with feeding customer activity data into HubSpot, such as website visits, form submissions, or campaign engagement metrics. HubSpot's built-in connectors cover many common tools, but engineers are often needed to maintain custom integrations or ensure that large volumes of historical data are loaded correctly [71].

Microsoft Dynamics 365 takes a different approach by combining CRM and enterprise resource planning (ERP) into a single platform. This means engineers may be asked to provide data that goes beyond sales and marketing, such as supply chain, finance, or operations data. Dynamics integrates closely with Microsoft's Power Platform, so data engineers often work with tools like Power Automate or Power BI to create flows between systems [72].

Other CRMs such as Zoho CRM or Freshsales cater to smaller teams but pose the same challenges at a smaller scale: how to ensure the system has accurate, clean, and timely data. Even these platforms often need integration with external data sources such as e-commerce platforms, support ticketing systems, or marketing automation tools.

What matters for the data engineer is not memorizing the specifics of every CRM but understanding how they operate conceptually. CRMs depend on structured, reliable customer data, and it's the engineer's role to design the pipelines and integrations that keep these systems running.

Chapter 6
Build or Buy?

"Don't reinvent the wheel, just realign it."

– Anthony J. D'Angelo [73]

When to Build, When to Buy

One of the most strategic decisions that data engineers and their organizations face is whether to build their own infrastructure or adopt vendor solutions. This, in addition to being a technical question, will rely on the budget, staffing, long-term strategy, and/or even the company's culture.

The DIY route gives organizations complete control over their infrastructure. Engineers can fine-tune the design, build custom logic tailored to business-specific use cases, and integrate tightly with internal systems. This approach is attractive to companies that operate at a scale or complexity not well served by off-the-shelf solutions. For example, Netflix famously built its own orchestration platform, Conductor, because existing tools did not meet its scale and reliability requirements [74].

DIY also helps avoid vendor lock-in, giving organizations more control over costs and the freedom to pivot without being bound to a provider's roadmap. However, this freedom comes at a price. Building in-house requires dedicated engineering teams to manage infrastructure, address scaling issues, handle upgrades, and provide ongoing support. What begins as a tailored solution can quickly become a long-term maintenance burden. The hidden cost of DIY is not just initial development, but the years of staff time spent keeping systems running.

Vendors like Snowflake, Databricks, Fivetran, and Stitch offer turnkey solutions that solve common data challenges out of the box. With these platforms, organizations can have a functioning pipeline in days instead of months. Vendors also handle scaling, uptime, and compliance certifications, which would be expensive and time-consuming to replicate internally. For smaller teams or fast-growing startups, vendor solutions allow engineers to focus on delivering insights instead of building infrastructure.

At the same time, vendor reliance comes with its own set of negatives, like pricing spikes based on consumption, being locked into features tied to the vendor's roadmaps, and lack of mobility if you wanted to switch off.

In practice, many organizations choose a hybrid model. They might use Fivetran to ingest common data sources, while writing custom extractors for niche systems. They may warehouse data in Snowflake but run transformations in dbt with homegrown testing frameworks. Hybrid approaches balance convenience and flexibility: teams lean on vendors for the basics while retaining control over the areas that give them competitive advantage.

For example, Airbnb initially relied heavily on open-source tools like Apache Hive and Facebook's PrestoDB, but later integrated vendor offerings for ease of scaling [75]. On the flip side, start-ups often start with vendor solutions to move quickly, then replace them with DIY systems as they grow and their needs become more complex.

The decision between building in-house or adopting a vendor solution is rarely straightforward, but a few guiding questions can help. First, do we have the engineering capacity to maintain this long term? If not, vendor solutions often make more sense. Second, is there a product that already solves 80–90% of our use case? If so, adopting it may save months of development. Finally, what is the total cost of ownership over three to five years, including licensing, cloud costs, staffing, and the opportunity cost of engineering time? In practice, the best approach is often a blend of both.

Chapter 7

Pipelining the Agile Way

"Plans are worthless, but planning is everything."

– Dwight D. Eisenhower [76]

Written Documentation

In data engineering, good documentation is as critical as clean code or reliable pipelines. Without clear documentation, even the most sophisticated data systems can quickly become difficult to understand, maintain, or extend. Documentation serves as the blueprint that explains how data flows through a system, why certain design decisions were made, and how to troubleshoot when issues arise, benefiting both current team members and future engineers. Effective documentation will offer context, explain dependencies, outline assumptions, and highlight known limitations. For data engineers, documenting pipelines, schemas, data sources, and transformation logic is essential to keeping data trustworthy, maintainable, and accessible throughout the organization.

Written documentation is a must in data engineering projects. It captures the reasoning behind design choices, outlines how systems are intended to work, and provides guidance for troubleshooting. Platforms like Atlassian's Confluence, Notion, Microsoft Word, and Google Docs are widely used because they can offer centralized access, collaborative editing, and powerful search capabilities. These platforms allow teams to create dedicated spaces or pages for project overviews, ETL pipeline designs, data dictionaries, onboarding guides, and runbooks for operational tasks. The exact implementation and tools you have available to you will depend on your specific organization, but the core ideas remain the same.

SOURCE IT

To make the framework for effective documentation easy to remember, I created the acronym SOURCE IT: Single Source, Organize, Update, Reasoning, Context, Examples, Integrate, and Trim. It captures the core principles I've found most useful for writing effective documentation as a data engineer. Each part of the SOURCE IT framework plays a role in ensuring documentation remains clear, useful, and sustainable over time. Let's walk through each principle to see how it applies in practice.

S - Single Source

A common issue in documentation is duplication. When the same piece of information exists in multiple places, it inevitably becomes inconsistent as updates happen in one location but not the other. A single source of truth (SSOT) means there is only one authoritative location for any given piece of information.

Imagine a team maintaining a data ingestion pipeline where connection details for a production database are documented in two separate places: a shared Google Doc, and a Confluence page. If any implementation details change and the engineer responsible only updates the documentation that she is familiar with, someone will eventually rely on the outdated copy and potentially break the pipeline.

Maintaining a SSOT also saves time. Engineers no longer have to search through multiple documents or Slack threads to verify details, and onboarding new team members becomes far simpler. The key is to choose the right central location for your documentation, make it accessible to everyone who needs it, and ensure that changes go through a clear update process. Once a SSOT is in place, trust in the documentation increases, and the team can focus more on solving problems rather than chasing down the right information.

O - Organize

Once you've established a single source of truth, the next step is to ensure that this information is presented in a way that people can actually use, removing any unnecessary guesswork. Even the most accurate and up-to-date documentation loses its value if it's buried in a maze of poorly structured pages.

A strong organizational structure often mirrors the systems you work with. You might have high-level categories for ingestion pipelines, transformation logic, data models, and monitoring. Within each category, keep your sections consistent in format, naming, and level of detail. If one page describes a process with diagrams, examples, and step-by-step instructions, the next similar page should follow the same pattern. This consistency builds familiarity and makes the documentation easier to navigate over time.

U - Update

Good organization makes documentation easy to find, but keeping it accurate is what makes it worth trusting. Outdated documentation can be worse than having no documentation at all because it misleads people into making decisions based on incorrect information. As a data engineer, your systems will evolve. Pipelines will be refactored, schemas will change, and tools will be replaced. Your documentation needs to evolve alongside them.

Updating should be a routine part of your workflow, not something left for "when there is time." Whenever you make a significant change to a system, process, or dataset, the corresponding documentation should be revised immediately. This can be made easier by linking documentation updates to your development workflow, such as requiring a documentation review as part of a pull request or deployment checklist.

A good habit is to periodically audit your documentation for accuracy. Schedule quarterly or biannual reviews where you or your team verify that every page still reflects reality. Even if nothing has changed, a quick confirmation ensures the content remains trustworthy. By keeping your documentation up to date, you maintain its role as the reliable backbone of your single source of truth.

R - Reasoning

Updating documentation keeps it accurate, but accuracy alone is not enough. Good documentation should also explain why decisions were made, not just what was done. Without this context, future readers may understand the current state of a system but have no insight into the thought process behind it. This can lead to repeating past mistakes or undoing design choices that were made for valid reasons.

In data engineering, reasoning is often tied to trade-offs. Perhaps a specific database was chosen because of its query performance under certain workloads, or a pipeline was designed a certain way to minimize costs. By recording these rationales, you give future engineers the ability to evaluate whether those reasons still apply and to make informed changes.

When writing documentation, ask yourself: If I came back to this project a year from now, would I know why this was built this way?

C - Context

While reasoning explains why something was done, context tells the reader where it fits within the bigger picture. Data engineering projects rarely exist in isolation. A pipeline might depend on an upstream system for input data, feed into multiple downstream processes, or be part of a larger initiative spanning several teams. Without this context, someone reading the documentation might understand the technical details but miss how the work connects to the organization's broader goals and systems.

Providing context could mean including diagrams that show how a data flow interacts with other components, noting which business teams rely on the output, or explaining how a specific dataset aligns with regulatory requirements. Even seemingly small bits of information such as which environment a script runs in or which API version it depends on, can save hours of troubleshooting later.

Context turns isolated knowledge into actionable knowledge. It ensures that engineers can make changes without unintentionally breaking something outside their immediate scope, and it helps new team members quickly orient themselves in a complex environment.

E - Examples

Examples turn abstract descriptions into something concrete and actionable. A well-chosen example can illustrate exactly how to use a query, call an API, or run a transformation job far better than paragraphs of explanation alone. For instance, instead of simply stating that a script "filters inactive accounts," you might show the exact command with the parameters used and the expected output. This allows readers to replicate your process with minimal guesswork.

Good examples should match real-world usage as closely as possible. They should reflect actual data shapes, realistic edge cases, and the most common scenarios a data engineer might encounter. If a process has multiple variations, documenting at least one example for each major use case can help cover the spectrum of possible situations.

By including examples, you remove ambiguity and make your documentation more approachable. Someone should be able to copy, adapt, and run your example with minimal changes, giving them immediate confidence that they understand the process.

I - Integrate

Documentation should not be a separate chore that lives outside the day-to-day work of a data engineer. The best documentation practices make writing and updating docs a natural part of your workflow. For example, when committing code changes to a repository, you could update the README or related Confluence page at the same time.

One of the main benefits of integrating documentation into your workflow is that you capture details while they are still fresh in your mind. The moment you finish implementing a feature, debugging a tricky issue, or configuring a system, you know exactly what you did and why you did it. Writing documentation at this point is faster, more accurate, and less likely to omit important context. Waiting even a few days can make you forget key steps or decisions, which can lead to incomplete or unclear records.

Integrating documentation into your existing processes also keeps it relevant. Schema changes can be documented directly in version control alongside migration scripts. Data quality checks can be annotated within monitoring tools. Even commit messages and code comments can serve as valuable, immediate documentation if they follow a consistent style.

These creations and updates should be part of your normal work rather than an optional afterthought, ensuring accuracy, usefulness, and ease of use. This approach fosters a culture where keeping documentation current is simply "how things are done."

T - Trim

Good documentation is not about writing as much as possible. It's about making sure the right information is clear, concise, and easy to find. Overly long or cluttered documents can discourage people from reading them, especially if they must dig through irrelevant details to find what they need. The goal is to present enough context for understanding without overwhelming the reader.

Trimming documentation involves removing outdated content, redundant explanations, and unnecessary tangents. If a process has changed, delete the old steps rather than leaving them in with a note "no longer used." If a long explanation can be summarized into a few bullet points or a short paragraph without losing meaning, simplify it. Where possible, link to additional resources instead of embedding large blocks of text.

Another aspect of trimming is organizing the document so the most important information appears first. This helps readers find critical instructions quickly while still allowing them to explore details if needed. Visual aids like tables, code snippets, and diagrams (which we will touch upon in the next section) can also replace lengthy descriptions, making the documentation more approachable.

A trimmed document is easier to maintain and more pleasant to use. People are far more likely to trust and rely on concise, well-structured documentation than on bloated pages that feel like a chore to navigate.

Visual Documentation

While written documentation forms the backbone of knowledge sharing, modern data engineers increasingly rely on visual documentation to complement it. In complex data environments, visuals often communicate ideas faster and more clearly than text alone. Data pipelines, architectural diagrams, and flowcharts can illustrate relationships, dependencies, and processes in a way that words cannot easily match.

For a data engineer, this is especially valuable when dealing with large-scale systems that have many moving parts. A visual pipeline diagram can show the flow of data from ingestion to storage to analytics at a glance, making it easier for both technical and non-technical stakeholders to understand the big picture. Similarly, entity relationship diagrams can map database schemas in a way that quickly reveals table relationships and dependencies.

Visual documentation also bridges communication gaps in collaborative environments. Teams working across different time zones or specializations can use these diagrams as a shared reference, ensuring that everyone understands how data moves through the system and where key transformations occur. In many cases, a well-designed diagram can prevent misunderstandings that might take several paragraphs of text to clarify.

By combining written and visual documentation, data engineers can create a more complete and accessible knowledge base. Text can provide detailed instructions, while visuals can guide readers through high-level concepts and complex system flows. Together, they form a richer documentation strategy that supports the fast-paced, collaborative nature of modern data engineering.

Entity Relationship Diagrams

Entity Relationship Diagrams (ERDs) are a foundational tool for documenting how data is structured in relational databases. They show the entities (tables) in a system, the attributes (columns) they contain, and the relationships between those entities. For a data engineer, ERDs act as a map that explains where data lives, how it connects, and what constraints or dependencies exist.

An ERD can prevent costly mistakes in pipeline development by making relationships clear before any SQL is written. For example, if you know that the orders table is linked to the customers table by a foreign key, you can design your ingestion and transformation logic to preserve referential integrity. Similarly, ERDs help when onboarding new engineers, since they offer a visual shorthand for the database schema without requiring a deep dive into every table's Data Definition Language (DDL).

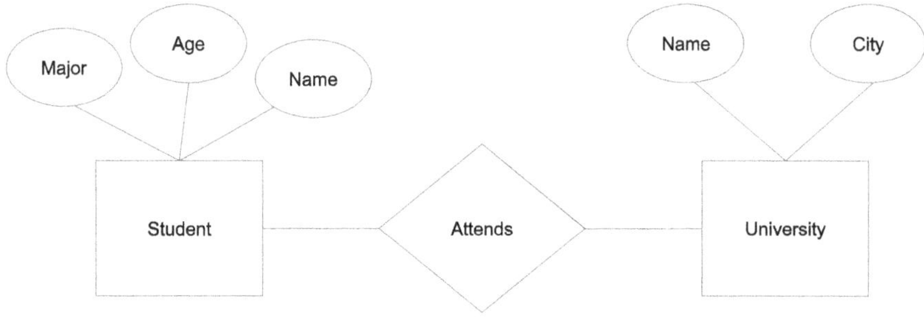

Figure 15: A Simple ERD Diagram

In practice, ERDs are especially helpful during database design, schema migrations, or when integrating data from multiple sources. They also serve as a reference point for analytics teams, making it easier for them to join tables correctly and avoid redundant queries. Tools like dbdiagram.io, Lucidchart, and MySQL Workbench can automatically generate ERDs from an existing database, while also allowing manual editing to add business-specific annotations.

Data Flow Diagrams

Data Flow Diagrams (DFDs) illustrate how data moves through a system, from its sources to its destinations, and the processes it passes through along the way. Unlike ERDs, which focus on data structure, DFDs emphasize the movement and transformation of data. For a data engineer, they are an effective way to visualize the entire lifecycle of data within a pipeline or application.

A typical DFD will show data sources (such as APIs, databases, or flat files), the processes that transform or enrich the data, and the storage locations or systems where the data eventually resides. Arrows indicate the flow between these components, making it easy to trace where a specific piece of information originated and where it will end up. This is particularly valuable when troubleshooting pipeline issues, since the diagram highlights each step where data could be delayed, altered, or lost.

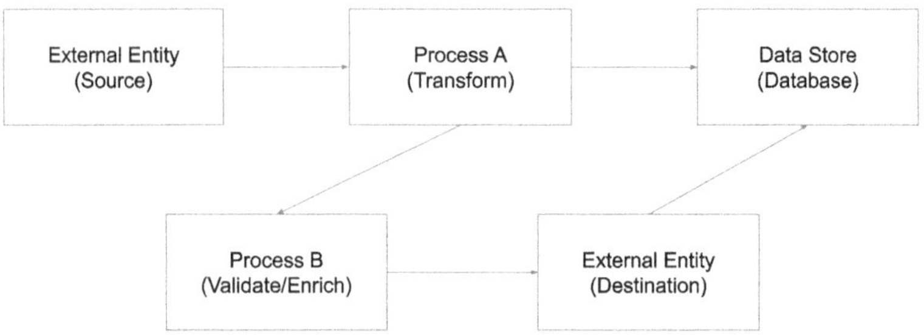

Figure 16: A Simple Data Flow Diagram

For example, in a modern ETL process, a DFD might show raw log data flowing from an S3 bucket into a Spark processing job, then being loaded into a Snowflake warehouse, and finally being consumed by a BI tool like Microsoft Power BI. By mapping these steps visually, the data engineer can spot unnecessary bottlenecks, redundant transformations, or opportunities to parallelize tasks for better performance.

System Architecture Diagrams

System architecture graphs provide a high-level view of how different components in a data ecosystem fit together. They show not just the flow of data, but also the infrastructure, services, and dependencies that make up the entire system. For a modern data engineer, these diagrams are invaluable for understanding how pipelines interact with storage systems, processing engines, APIs, and end-user applications.

Unlike DFD, which focuses specifically on the path data takes, system architecture graphs reveal the broader environment in which the data pipeline operates. For instance, a cloud-based architecture diagram might show event streaming services like Kafka feeding into processing frameworks such as Apache Spark, with storage in Snowflake or BigQuery, all connected to orchestration tools and visualized in BI platforms like Looker. This top-down view helps engineers, architects, and stakeholders quickly grasp the relationships and dependencies between systems.

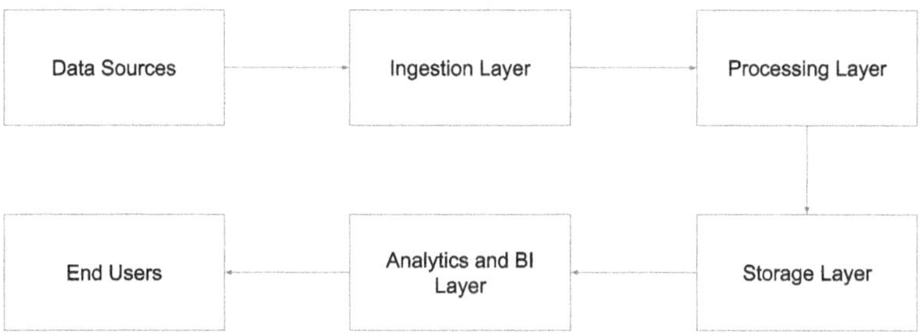

Figure 17: A Simple System Architecture Diagram

These diagrams help identify single points of failure, security boundaries, and integration points. In a large enterprise setting, a system architecture graph can highlight which services are managed in-house, which are hosted in the cloud, and how network boundaries or VPNs affect connectivity. This is crucial for planning infrastructure changes, scaling resources, or diagnosing systemic issues.

Dependency Graphs

Dependency graphs map out the relationships between different components, datasets, or processes in a system. For a data engineer, they are particularly useful for showing how upstream changes ripple through a pipeline and where downstream systems depend on specific data or transformations. This visibility is crucial when troubleshooting failures, planning schema changes, or assessing the impact of removing or replacing a system component.

In practice, a dependency graph might illustrate how a raw data source flows into multiple transformation jobs, which in turn feed into analytics tables or machine learning models. By following the edges in the graph, a data engineer can quickly see which jobs will fail if a source becomes unavailable, or which datasets will be affected by a breaking change in a transformation script. This level of clarity is essential for reducing risk during deployments and for ensuring business continuity.

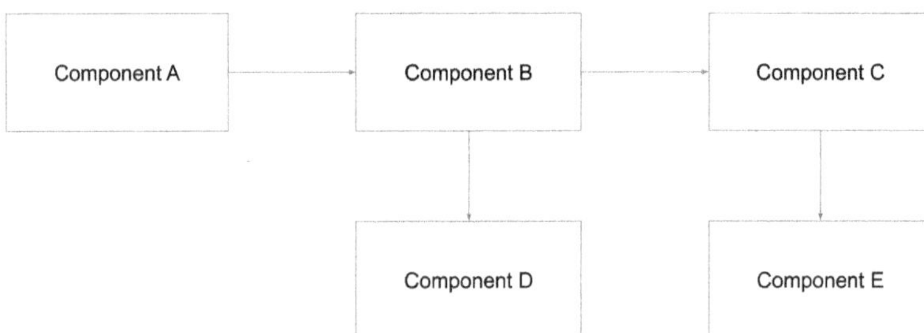

Figure 18: A Simple Dependency Graph

Dependency graphs are also valuable for optimization. By examining the connections, engineers can identify redundant processing steps, spot unnecessary joins or lookups, and consolidate workloads. Over time, this can lead to more efficient pipelines and reduced infrastructure costs.

Visual documentation is only as effective as the tools that bring it to life. For entity relationship diagrams, tools like Lucidchart, dbdiagram.io, or draw.io make it easy to map database structures. Data flow diagrams can be created in platforms such as Microsoft Visio, Miro, or even Google Slides for lightweight collaboration. System architecture graphs benefit from diagramming tools like Cacoo or diagrams.net, while dependency graphs can be produced using orchestration tool visualizations such as Apache Airflow, dbt, or custom Graphviz outputs. Selecting the right tool for each type of diagram ensures clarity while making it easier to keep documentation up to date, reinforcing its value as a core resource for modern data engineering teams.

Code and Repository-Level Documentation

At the code level, clear docstrings, inline comments, and usage examples ensure that others can follow the logic without needing to dissect every line. Standards like Google's Python Style Guide or PEP 257 help maintain consistency, making it easier for multiple engineers to work in the same codebase. This is especially valuable for shared ETL scripts, transformation logic, or orchestration workflows, where the reasoning behind each step should be immediately apparent.

At the repository level, documentation serves as the first point of contact for anyone new to the project. A strong README should explain the project's purpose, installation steps, configuration details, and usage examples. More complex repositories may benefit from additional files covering API references, architectural overviews, or troubleshooting guides. Specifically for data engineering work, it should also detail data sources, dependencies, and environment setup so that workflows can be reproduced with minimal friction.

Several tools can streamline documentation efforts. Sphinx, MkDocs, and Docusaurus can generate polished documentation sites directly from docstrings and markdown files. GitHub and GitLab make it easy to maintain READMEs and project wikis, while linters like pydocstyle or flake8-docstrings enforce consistent formatting. Studying other well-documented open-source projects can provide practical examples of effective documentation structures. By making documentation a priority both in code and at the repository level, data engineers can ensure that their code remains clear, scalable, and accessible long after the initial build.

Whatever platform or tool you choose for documentation, take the time to learn its built-in features. Most documentation platforms offer search functions, tagging, version history, and templates that can make your work more organized and easier to navigate. Leveraging these capabilities will help you spend less time formatting and more time adding meaningful content.

Documentation should not be a solo effort. Encourage teammates to contribute their own notes, clarifications, and updates. When others document their work, it strengthens the overall knowledge base and benefits you directly by providing answers and context you might need later.

Agile and Scrum Workflows

In the world of technology, how work gets done can be just as important as the work itself. For decades, teams relied on rigid, sequential processes to build software, develop systems, and deliver data solutions. These approaches worked well when problems were well defined, and the environment surrounding a project was relatively stable. But as the pace of innovation accelerated, and as data became central to decision-making, many of those traditional processes began to show their cracks.

Data engineers, in particular, operate in a space where requirements rarely stand still. New data sources appear, pipelines must adapt, and business needs often shift before a project is even halfway complete. Under older approaches, this kind of constant change could derail entire timelines, leaving teams frustrated and stakeholders disappointed. It became clear that the industry needed a way to work that embraced change instead of resisting it.

This is where Agile and Scrum come in. More than just buzzwords, these methodologies represent a shift in mindset: moving from lengthy, rigid cycles to shorter, iterative ones where feedback is frequent and teams stay adaptable. For a data engineer, this shift can mean the difference between delivering a pipeline that is already outdated at launch, and delivering one that evolves smoothly alongside business needs.

Before Agile became the standard, many teams relied on the Waterfall model for managing projects. Waterfall is one of the earliest structured approaches to software development, and it gets its name from the way work flows in one direction, much like a waterfall cascading down. Each stage of the project is completed fully before moving on to the next. Requirements are gathered, then design is completed, then development, then testing, and finally deployment. Once a stage is finished, teams rarely go back to make changes, which gives the process its linear, step-by-step structure. The methodology originates from computer scientist Winston Royce's 1970 paper, *Managing the Development of Large Software Systems* [77]. While the term 'waterfall' is never explicitly mentioned, waterfall methodology is widely credited toward this paper.

Waterfall Approach

The Waterfall approach brought clarity to projects in its time, as managers could easily track progress by knowing which stage a team was in. It also worked well for industries where requirements were stable and unlikely to change, such as manufacturing or construction. However, when applied to software and data projects, it often struggled. Requirements in technology are rarely static, and the inability to adapt quickly meant that teams could end up delivering products that no longer met user needs by the time they were complete.

Figure 19: The Waterfall Approach

Imagining a workflow where requirements for pipelines, storage solutions, or APIs were locked in at the beginning highlights the rigidity of Waterfall. If new data sources became available halfway through, or if business needs shifted, a strict Waterfall process would make it difficult to incorporate those changes. This limitation is one of the key reasons why the industry began to shift toward more adaptive methods like Agile, where iteration and flexibility are central.

Although the Waterfall model has fallen out of favor in

fast-moving technology teams, it has not disappeared. It's still used in industries where predictability, documentation, and regulatory compliance are critical. Fields like aerospace, healthcare, and government contracting often require extensive upfront planning and approvals, which align with Waterfall's structured stages. In these contexts, the cost of change can be extremely high, so a rigid model provides more control. Even within software, Waterfall might be used for projects with very clear and stable requirements, such as implementing a well-defined reporting system or migrating data from one platform to another without introducing new features. While not suited to every project, Waterfall remains an option in situations where clarity and control outweigh flexibility.

What is Agile methodology?

Agile methodology is a way of working that emphasizes adaptability, collaboration, and delivering value in smaller, more manageable increments. Instead of committing to a fixed plan at the start of a project, Agile encourages teams to work in short cycles, constantly reviewing progress and adjusting priorities as new information emerges. This flexibility makes it particularly well-suited for technology projects, where requirements often evolve and customer needs can change rapidly.

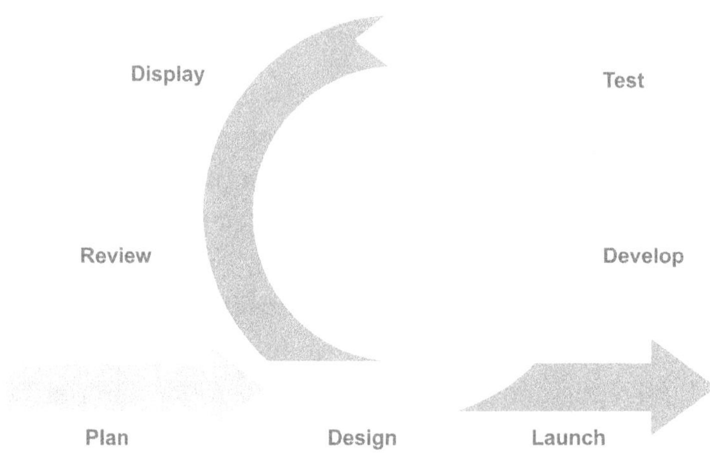

Figure 20: The Agile Approach

The goal of Agile is to shorten the time between identifying a need and delivering a working solution. By breaking projects into smaller pieces, teams can release usable components faster, gather feedback, and incorporate that feedback into the next cycle. This reduces the risk of building something that no longer meets the business need by the time it is finished. Agile also encourages closer communication among team members and stakeholders, which helps to uncover issues early and resolve them before they grow into larger problems.

The benefits of this approach are significant. Agile makes it easier to respond to changing requirements, improves transparency between technical and business teams, and creates opportunities to deliver value sooner rather than later. Teams that follow Agile often see higher-quality outcomes because they test and refine their work continuously instead of waiting until the end of a long project cycle. For data engineers specifically, this could mean deploying a small but working pipeline that ingests a single data source, then expanding it over time, instead of attempting to build a complex system all at once. For other roles, such as developers, product managers, or analysts, it may mean prioritizing the features that deliver the most impact early, while staying ready to pivot as needs shift.

Agile shouldn't be viewed as a single framework but rather a philosophy that can be applied in many different ways. Scrum, Kanban, Lean, and Extreme Programming are all frameworks that embody Agile principles in different forms. What unites them is the focus on delivering value continuously, empowering teams to make decisions, and ensuring that feedback loops are built into the process. While Agile began in software development, it has since spread to many other industries, from finance to marketing to healthcare, because its benefits extend well beyond coding.

Scrum Methodology and Ceremonies

Scrum is the most widely adopted Agile framework, and its popularity comes from its simplicity and clear structure. It was first formalized in literary form called the Scrum Guide in the mid-1990s by

Jeff Sutherland and Ken Schwaber, who drew inspiration from earlier work on lightweight project management techniques and from a 1986 Harvard Business Review article by Hirotaka Takeuchi and Ikujiro Nonaka, two prominent Japanese organizational theorists, comparing high-performing product development teams to a rugby scrum, where players work tightly together to move the ball down the field [78]. The name "Scrum" was chosen because it reflects this same idea of close collaboration, teamwork, and continuous forward progress [79].

What makes Scrum unique is its emphasis on well-defined roles, events, and artifacts that guide the team's workflow. The framework is built around short, fixed-length cycles called sprints, typically lasting two to four weeks. Each sprint produces a potentially shippable increment of work, which ensures that progress is both measurable and aligned with stakeholder needs. This incremental delivery model helps teams adapt quickly to changes in requirements, while still maintaining a sense of structure and predictability.

Scrum is also distinctive in the way it distributes responsibility. It establishes three primary roles: the Product Owner, who is responsible for prioritizing work based on business value; the Scrum Master, who facilitates the process and removes obstacles; and the Development Team, which is self-organizing and responsible for delivering the actual work. Unlike traditional project management approaches, Scrum places a strong emphasis on empowering the team rather than relying on top-down control. This empowerment encourages accountability, creativity, and continuous improvement.

Another unique feature of Scrum is its focus on transparency and inspection. The framework defines several key meetings, often called ceremonies, that structure the work and keep the team aligned. We will touch on a few of these ceremonies in the following paragraphs.

Daily Scrum (Stand-up)

This is a short, time-boxed meeting of usually 15 minutes, held every day of the sprint. Each team member shares what they worked on yesterday, what they plan to do today, and whether they face any blockers. The purpose is not to report to a manager but to synchronize as a team and spot obstacles early. If deeper conversations are needed, they happen after the stand-up to keep the meeting focused.

Sprint Planning

At the start of each sprint, the team meets to decide what work can realistically be completed in the upcoming cycle. The Product Owner presents the prioritized backlog items, and the team discusses them to clarify requirements, estimate effort, and commit to a sprint goal. By the end of the session, everyone has a shared understanding of the sprint's objectives and the specific tasks to be delivered.

Sprint Review

At the end of a sprint, the team demonstrates the completed work to stakeholders. This is an opportunity to gather feedback, confirm that the output meets expectations, and adjust priorities if needed. The focus is on the product increment and how it moves the project forward.

Sprint Retrospective

This meeting follows the sprint review and looks inward at the team's process. The group reflects on what went well, what challenges they faced, and how they can improve in the next sprint. Retrospectives encourage continuous improvement and help teams adapt not just their product, but their way of working.

Together, these meetings create a rhythm of planning, execution, review, and improvement. They ensure that the team stays aligned, issues are surfaced quickly, and both the product and the process evolve in response to feedback.

Scrum's origins in software development have not limited its reach. Today, it's used in data engineering, product design, marketing, and even in fields outside of technology. Its lightweight structure makes it appealing to teams of all sizes and disciplines, especially those working in fast-paced environments where priorities change often. By combining clear rules with flexibility, Scrum has become the de facto way for many organizations to bring Agile to life.

Kanban Methodology

While Scrum emphasizes fixed-length sprints and structured ceremonies, the Kanban methodology focuses on visualizing the flow of work and limiting the amount of work in progress at any given time. At the heart of this approach is the Kanban board, a tool designed to make work visible and help teams manage priorities effectively.

To Do	In Progress	Done
Create slide deck	Test error handling	Conduct code walkthrough with new employee
Research ingestion tools	Implement incremental load	
	Run Spark job performance benchmarks	

Figure 21: A Simple Kanban Board

A Kanban board is usually divided into columns that represent different stages of work. The most basic setup includes "To Do," "In Progress," and "Done." As tasks move from one stage to another, they are represented as cards that progress across the board. This simple visual framework makes it easy for the team to see what is being worked on, where bottlenecks are forming, and how close the team is to completing tasks.

Another key aspect of Kanban is the concept of limiting work in progress (often referred to as WIP limits). By restricting how many tasks can be in a column at once, teams are encouraged to finish work before starting something new. This encourages throughput, reduces context switching and keeps quality high.

Kanban boards can be physical (with sticky notes on a wall) or digital (using tools like Jira, Trello, or Azure DevOps). Digital boards are often more practical since they can integrate with code repositories, CI/CD pipelines, and issue tracking systems. This integration helps the board stay up to date automatically and ensures that the status of work is always transparent to the team.

Kanban is particularly useful in environments where work arrives unpredictably, such as production support or operational tasks. Unlike Scrum, which organizes work into planned sprints, Kanban allows for a continuous flow of work. This makes it an excellent complement to Scrum in many organizations, especially when both planned project work and unplanned requests need to be handled [80].

Extreme Programming

Extreme Programming, often abbreviated as XP, is another Agile methodology that emphasizes high-quality software and rapid responsiveness to changing requirements. While Scrum focuses on process and ceremonies, XP is more concerned with technical practices and engineering discipline. It was introduced in the late 1990s by computer scientist Kent Beck, who sought to improve software quality and make development more adaptable in fast-changing environments [81].

At its core, XP promotes values such as simplicity, communication, feedback, courage, and respect. These values are reinforced through a set of concrete practices that differentiate XP from other Agile frameworks. For example, pair programming encourages two developers to work together at one workstation, ensuring constant code review and knowledge sharing. Test-driven development (TDD) requires writing automated tests before writing the actual code, which helps maintain quality and reduce defects. Continuous integration (CI) is another hallmark of XP, where code changes are merged and tested frequently, sometimes multiple times a day, to ensure stability and detect problems early.

XP also emphasizes customer involvement. Similar to Scrum's Product Owner role, XP requires close collaboration with the customer, often in the form of an on-site customer who can provide feedback, clarify requirements, and prioritize features in real time. This ensures that the team is always working on what delivers the most value.

While XP was once considered "radical" for its heavy reliance on practices like pair programming and TDD, many of its ideas have since become mainstream in modern software development. Continuous integration, automated testing, and iterative development are now standard in many engineering teams, even if they do not adopt XP formally.

Tools for Agile Development

Adopting Agile or Scrum requires tools that can support collaboration, visibility, and accountability. While teams can implement these frameworks with something as simple as a whiteboard and sticky notes, most organizations use digital platforms to manage projects at scale. These tools provide transparency across distributed teams, enable tracking of progress, and integrate with development pipelines.

Jira

Jira, developed by Atlassian, is perhaps the most widely used tool for managing Agile and Scrum workflows. It allows teams to create and track user stories, epics, and tasks, all organized on boards that can be customized for Scrum or Kanban. Sprint planning becomes straightforward: teams can assign story points, prioritize backlog items, and then track sprint progress through burndown charts and velocity reports. Jira also integrates seamlessly with development tools like Bitbucket, GitHub, and CI/CD pipelines, which makes it useful for data engineers and software developers working in fast-moving environments [82].

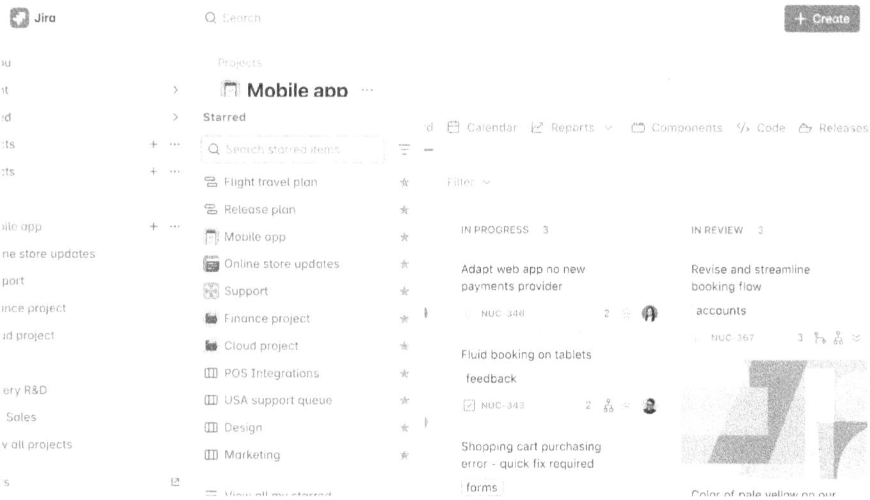

Figure 22: An Example User's Jira View [83]

Trello

Trello is another popular tool, known for its simplicity and visual Kanban-style boards. Teams can create lists and cards to represent tasks and move them across columns like "To Do," "In Progress," and "Done." While Trello doesn't have all the advanced features of Jira, It's easy to adopt and highly flexible, making it appealing to smaller teams or organizations just starting with Agile [84].

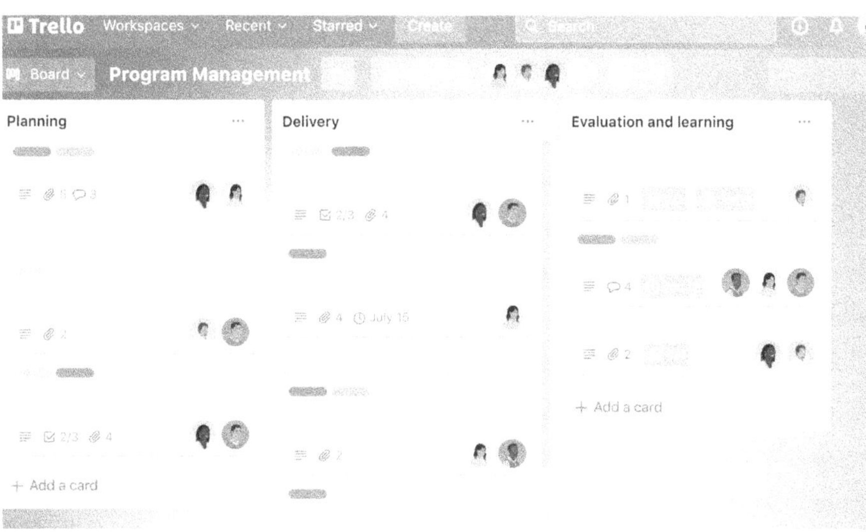

Figure 23: An Example User's Trello View [85]

Asana

Asana provides a broader project management suite that supports both Agile and non-Agile workflows. It allows teams to visualize work in Kanban boards, Gantt charts, or calendars, making it useful for organizations that need to manage cross-functional projects. Data engineers might use Asana to track ETL pipeline improvements while also collaborating with analysts or business stakeholders on reporting initiatives [86].

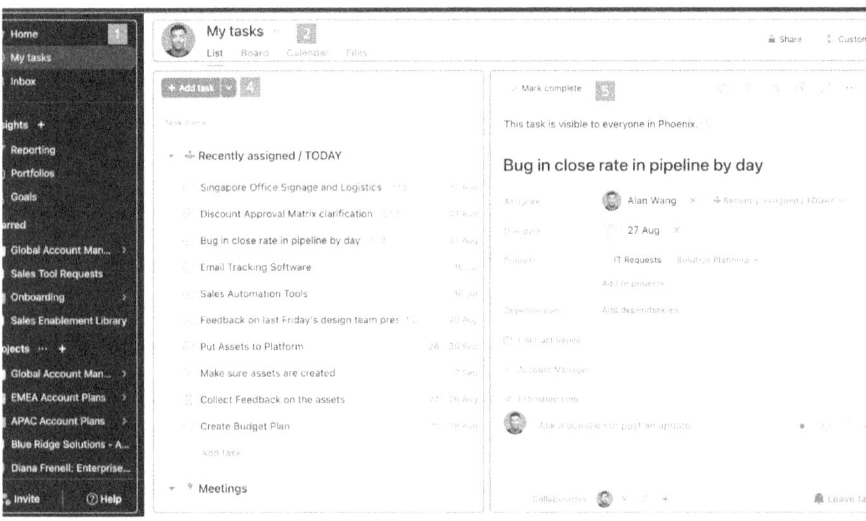

Figure 24: An Example User's Asana View [87]

Azure DevOps

For teams working heavily within Microsoft ecosystems, Azure DevOps provides built-in support for Scrum and Agile workflows. It includes backlog management, sprint planning, dashboards, and integration with CI/CD pipelines. It's particularly popular in enterprise environments where compliance and integration with other Microsoft services are important [88].

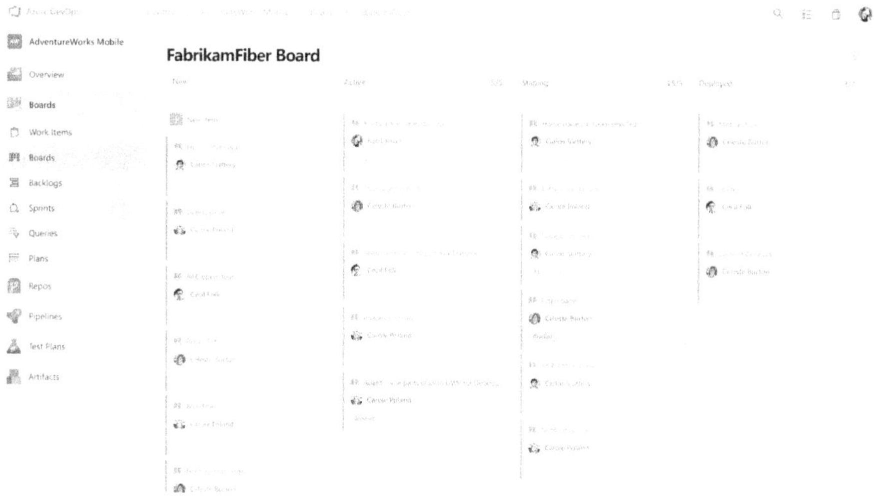

Figure 25: An Example User's Azure DevOps View [89]

GitHub Projects and GitLab Boards

Both GitHub and GitLab have added lightweight project management features that support Agile workflows. GitHub Projects, for instance, allows teams to create Kanban-style boards directly tied to issues and pull requests. This makes it easier to connect code changes to backlog items. GitLab Boards work similarly and integrate tightly with GitLab's CI/CD features, which can be beneficial for teams practicing continuous integration in line with XP principles.

Figure 26: An Example User's Gitlab Boards View [90]

Agility on a Budget

One of the biggest misconceptions about Agile and Scrum is that you need expensive enterprise-grade tools to make them work. In reality, Agile was designed to be lightweight, adaptable, and people-focused. For small teams or startups without a big software budget, there are many ways to practice Agile effectively without sacrificing quality or collaboration.

Whiteboards and Sticky Notes

For example, a simple whiteboard divided into To Do, In Progress, and Done with sticky notes can function as a powerful Kanban board. It provides instant visibility and is easy to update during stand-ups. Another few strong free options are Notion or Google Sheets. A shared spreadsheet with task columns can be surprisingly effective for sprint tracking. Notion takes this a step further, offering customizable Kanban boards, calendars, and integrated documentation.

A Systems Viewpoint

Systems thinking is a concept borrowed from the field of systems engineering. By definition, systems thinking encourages us to anticipate how a whole system will behave when its parts interact or enter new conditions. The goal is to spot emergent effects and unintended consequences early, then shape design and operations so the system handles change without surprises. In data work, that means holding the entire pipeline in your head at once—sources, ingestion, storage, transforms, serving, and monitoring—and asking how a change in one area will echo through the rest.

Begin by decomposing the platform into subsystems with crisp boundaries and purposes. Name the handoffs between them and be explicit about what each handoff carries: meaning, timing, and constraints. This framing makes side effects easier to reason about. If a product team redefines a "trial_user," you can trace where that meaning flows, which transforms depend on it, and which decisions downstream could shift. If a payment gateway adds retries, you can anticipate duplicate events, prepare idempotent transforms, and prevent inflated revenue metrics.

Keep situational awareness of both the internal and external environment. Internally, track schema intentions, SLAs, quotas, cost sensitivity, and who owns what. Externally, watch for seasonality, marketing pushes, regulatory changes, vendor updates, and organizational incentives that might change how source systems behave. A holiday sale can double event volume; a privacy policy update can restrict fields you assumed were stable; a partner rollout can move latency targets. With that awareness, you can model likely system responses rather than react after the fact.

Ask forward-looking "what if" questions before making changes. What if the new event field arrives late for part of the day? What if a consumer bypasses the semantic layer and queries raw logs? What if a region fails and traffic concentrates elsewhere? Then plan the safe path: stage the change where you can compare old and new outputs, pick a clear decision rule for cutover, and define the condition that triggers a revert. This is the same reasoning a systems engineer applies when breaking down a complex product like a self-driving car—identify subsystems, consider the environment they operate in, and think through how human behavior or edge conditions will push the system. For data engineers, that translates to anticipating producer quirks, consumer shortcuts, and real-world bursts so the platform behaves as expected when it meets reality.

The heart of Agile lies in practices, discipline, and communication, not in the software that supports them. Expensive software can make it easier to implement agile methodology because of its intuitive UI and extra features, but all you really need is a shared video call and tracking board (as simple as a set of sticky notes) to successfully plan or run daily stand-ups. What matters most is consistency and commitment from the team as a whole in the adoption of Agile practices.

Chapter 8

Errors, Errors, Errors

"If debugging is the process of removing software bugs, then programming must be the process of putting them in."

– Edsger Dijkstra [91]

Backups and Storage Systems

An important responsibility for a data engineer is ensuring that data is not only available in the moment but also safeguarded for the long term. Emergencies can strike at any time, and without reliable backups and thoughtful storage strategies, recovery may be impossible. Long-term storage and backup planning is therefore at the heart of resilience.

Data engineers have a wide variety of tools and approaches to choose from, each with its own strengths, costs, and trade-offs. At the simplest level, traditional full backups copy entire datasets to a safe location, providing a complete snapshot of the system at a given point in time. More efficient methods, like incremental and differential backups, reduce storage and time costs by only capturing what has changed. Beyond traditional backups, long-term archiving solutions, such as cold storage services, offer inexpensive ways to preserve data that may not be needed frequently but cannot be discarded.

Cloud providers have further expanded the toolkit. Snapshotting databases, replication across regions, and using write-ahead logs as a recovery mechanism are all practical options that engineers regularly employ. Choosing among these requires balancing cost, performance, and business requirements for recovery point objectives (RPO) and recovery time objectives (RTO).

Good backup and storage practices regularly test restores, maintain versioning to guard against silent corruption, and ensure compliance with data retention policies. A backup that has never been tested may not be a backup at all. In practice, resilient organizations treat backup and storage not as an afterthought but as a core feature of their pipelines.

Types of Backups

There are several strategies for backing up data, each offering a balance between reliability, cost, and speed. The most straightforward approach is a full backup, which creates a complete copy of all data at a specific point in time. Full backups are simple to restore since they contain everything in one place, but they can be slow to run and require significant storage space. To address these challenges, many organizations adopt incremental backups. Incremental backups only capture the data that has changed since the last backup, making them faster and more storage-efficient. However, restoring from incremental backups can take longer since multiple sets of changes need to be reapplied. A middle-ground approach is the differential backup, which saves all changes made since the last full backup. Differential backups require more storage than incrementals but make recovery quicker since only two backup sets are needed.

Archiving and Storage Tiers: Hot, Warm, and Cold

Not all data requires the same level of accessibility, and treating all data equally can be costly. Storage strategies typically fall into three tiers: hot, warm, and cold, each balancing speed, cost, and use case. Hot storage holds frequently accessed, real-time data at high cost and speed, warm storage balances cost and accessibility for occasionally used datasets, and cold storage provides the lowest-cost option for archiving historical or compliance data that is rarely accessed. We've already seen how hot storage systems like databases, Redis, or SSD-backed object stores keep operational data available in real time for dashboards, applications, and models. But as data ages or becomes less critical, it can be transitioned into cheaper, slower storage tiers.

Warm storage sits between hot and cold. It provides a balance of lower cost with moderate retrieval speed, making it a good fit for data that is queried occasionally but not constantly. Common examples include logs from the past 90 days, recent analytics datasets, or archived reports that may still need periodic review. Cloud providers offer services like Amazon S3 Standard-Infrequent Access or Azure Cool Blob Storage to serve this middle ground. Warm storage is often used as a staging layer, where data transitions from hot to cold once it becomes less relevant.

Cold storage is built for long-term retention at minimal cost. It is ideal for compliance-related or historical data that cannot be discarded but is rarely accessed, such as regulatory records, audit logs, or multi-year transaction histories. Retrieval times can range from minutes to hours, but the cost savings are significant. Examples include Amazon Glacier, Azure Archive Storage, and Google Coldline Storage. Cold storage strategies often include retention policies to ensure compliance. For instance, a financial institution may keep transaction logs for seven years, while web application logs might be retained for just three months.

Modern cloud platforms make managing these tiers easier through built-in lifecycle policies and automated backup features. Amazon S3, for example, supports lifecycle rules that automatically move objects between hot, warm, and cold storage classes based on access patterns, ensuring active data remains fast while older files transition to cheaper tiers [92]. Azure Blob Storage provides similar hot, cool, and archive options, while Google Cloud Storage offers comparable lifecycle rules that can move or even delete files after a set period [93].

Beyond object storage, cloud databases also provide automated backups and snapshots. Services may also allow engineers to enable point-in-time recovery, making disaster recovery much simpler. These features reduce the need for manual oversight, enforce retention policies automatically, and give organizations confidence that their data will remain both accessible and compliant without constant human intervention.

Fault-Tolerant Distributed Systems

At its core, a fault tolerant system is one that continues to operate correctly even when part of the system fails. Instead of collapsing under the weight of a hardware outage, a network partition, or a corrupted process, the system is designed to adapt, recover, and keep delivering its essential functions. In the world of data engineering, fault tolerance is not optional. Data pipelines, databases, and analytics platforms are often the lifeblood of an organization, and downtime can mean lost revenue, lost trust, or regulatory consequences.

A distributed system is one in which computation and storage are spread across multiple machines, often in different physical or geographical locations, but working together to appear as a single system to the end user. By combining many smaller, interconnected components rather than relying on a single machine, distributed systems unlock scalability, resilience, and flexibility. However, they also introduce challenges, since more moving parts mean more potential points of failure.

When these two concepts come together, we arrive at fault tolerant distributed systems: architectures designed to withstand both predictable and unpredictable failures without losing data or becoming unavailable. These systems replicate data across nodes, distribute computation in ways that can recover from interruptions, and maintain consensus even when some participants are offline. Fault tolerance in distributed systems ensures that failures do not bring the system down.

Redundancy

Redundancy is the cornerstone of fault tolerance. At its simplest, redundancy means having a backup plan: duplicate systems, components, or data copies that can take over when something fails. Without redundancy, any single failure could cascade into a system-wide outage. Redundancy is the difference between pipelines that stop at the first hiccup and pipelines that continue running even when individual parts of the infrastructure fail.

In practice, redundancy shows up at many levels. At the hardware level, servers might be equipped with multiple power supplies or network interfaces so that the failure of one component doesn't cause downtime. At the data level, information is often replicated across multiple disks, servers, or even entire data centers. A common example is RAID (Redundant Array of Independent Disks), where a controller manages data that is distributed across multiple drives so that if one fails, the system can continue functioning. RAID levels define how the data is arranged. RAID 0 splits files across disks (striping) to improve speed but offers no protection. RAID 1 duplicates data on multiple disks (mirroring) for reliability. RAID 5 and RAID 6 spread both data and backup information (parity) across disks, allowing the system to rebuild lost data if one or two drives fail, balancing performance and fault tolerance [94].

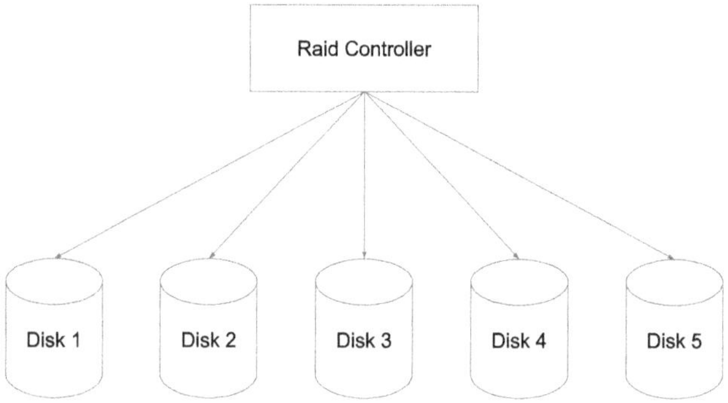

Figure 27: A Simple RAID Visualization

Redundancy also extends to infrastructure architecture. Virtually all of the cloud platforms that we have covered before encourage engineers to deploy systems across multiple availability zones within a region. This ensures that if one zone experiences issues like a power failure or a localized outage, the other zones can continue to serve traffic. For systems where downtime carries massive costs, redundancy may even involve multi-region deployment, where entire replicas of the application and its data exist in different geographic areas. This kind of redundancy allows services to withstand region-wide failures, which are rare but not impossible.

Of course, redundancy is not free. Duplicating data and infrastructure increases storage and compute costs, and it adds operational complexity. Engineers must carefully design replication strategies, monitor synchronization between redundant systems, and balance costs against risk. The key is to determine the level of redundancy appropriate for the system's importance. A small internal dashboard may not justify cross-region replication, but a production database supporting customer transactions almost certainly does.

Redundancy is therefore both a technical principle and a strategic decision. It provides resilience by ensuring that there is always another copy, another component, or another system ready to step in when failures occur. Mastering redundancy is one of the first steps in designing distributed systems that do not just scale but also survive.

Examples of Redundancy in Practice

- Netflix and Chaos Engineering

  Netflix is one of the most famous examples of engineering for resilience. The company runs its streaming platform on AWS and uses redundancy extensively to ensure users can always watch their shows, even if part of the system fails [95]. Content is replicated across multiple AWS regions, and services are deployed redundantly so that if one cluster goes down, others can pick up the load. To test this redundancy, Netflix created Chaos Monkey, a tool that intentionally terminates random servers to make sure the platform survives failures [96]. This culture of embracing redundancy and testing it regularly has become a best practice across the industry.
- AWS S3 Durability

  Amazon Simple Storage Service (S3) is designed with redundancy as its core promise. Amazon claims eleven nines of durability (99.999999999%) for objects stored in S3 [97]. This is achieved by redundantly storing data across multiple devices and facilities within an AWS region. Even if several disks or servers fail, the data remains safe. For critical applications, engineers can enable Cross-Region Replication (CRR), which stores data in another AWS region altogether, ensuring protection against regional outages [98].
- Kubernetes and Pod Replication

  At the infrastructure orchestration level, Kubernetes builds redundancy into how it manages workloads. Applications are deployed in "pods," and engineers can configure replication controllers or deployments to ensure a certain number of pod instances are always running. If one pod crashes, Kubernetes automatically spins up another to maintain redundancy. This ensures that applications remain available to users even when underlying hardware or nodes fail.

Replication

Replication is the deliberate act of creating and maintaining multiple copies of data across different machines or nodes in a distributed system. While redundancy ensures there are backups or spares ready in case of failure, replication is specifically about keeping those duplicates consistent and usable in real time. For fault tolerant systems, replication is one of the most important strategies because it directly protects both availability (data is always accessible) and durability (data is not lost, even when failures occur).

Replication strategies can differ depending on the system's priorities. In synchronous replication, updates are written to all replicas before confirming success to the client. This guarantees consistency but introduces latency, since every replica must acknowledge the change. By contrast, asynchronous replication allows the primary system to confirm the update immediately while

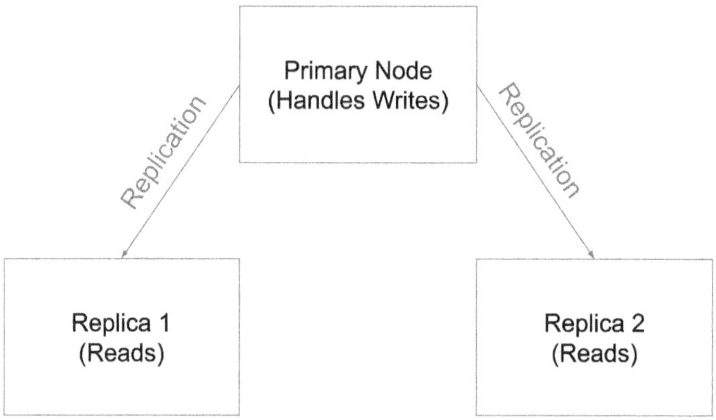

Figure 28: Primary-Replica Model

changes are propagated to replicas in the background. This approach improves performance and availability but risks temporary inconsistencies, often referred to as eventual consistency.

Different distributed systems take different stances on replication. Many traditional databases often use a primary-replica model, where one primary node handles all writes and propagates those changes to replicas. In the event of failure, a replica can be promoted to primary, ensuring continuity.

Many data stores are known as distributed databases, meaning that they use peer-to-peer replication, where multiple nodes can accept writes and coordinate to resolve conflicts. This design prioritizes availability and scalability, often at the cost of strict consistency.

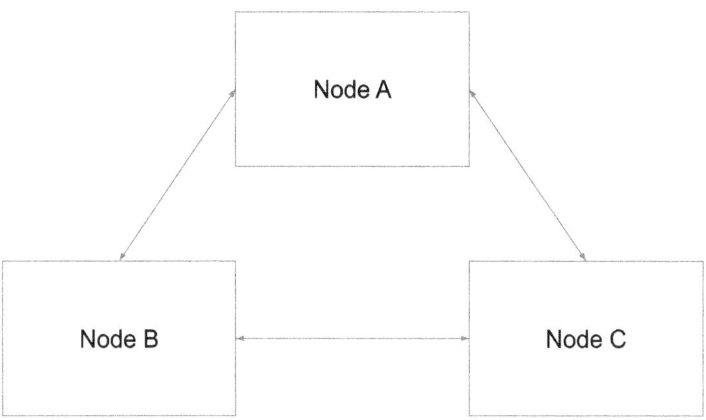

Figure 29: Peer-to-Peer Replication

Replication also ties into larger concepts like computer scientist Eric Brewer's CAP theorem, which states that a distributed system can only provide two of the three guarantees at any one time: consistency, availability, and partition tolerance [99], [100]. Replication strategies are often designed with these trade-offs in mind. For example, synchronous replication leans toward consistency, while asynchronous approaches lean toward availability. Understanding this balance is critical for data engineers who design

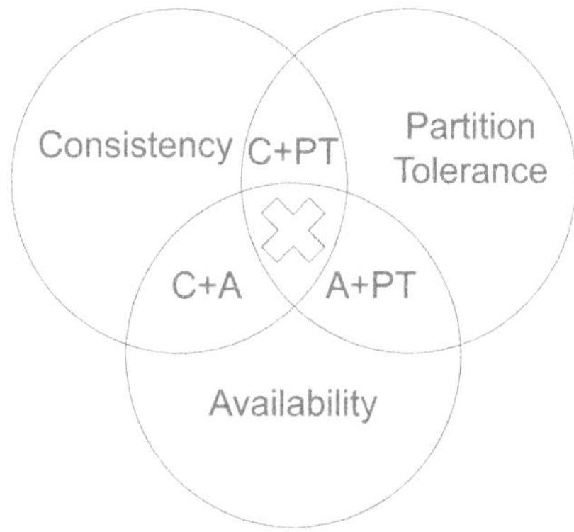

Figure 30: Brewer's CAP Theorem

systems to meet specific business needs.

In practice, replication allows many data stores to promise near-continuous uptime. These platforms replicate data across multiple zones and regions so that even if one region experiences downtime, users can still query their data with minimal interruption.

Real-World Examples of Replication

- Cassandra's Tunable Consistency

  Apache Cassandra, as we briefly mentioned before, is a distributed data store designed for high availability and scalability. What makes its replication strategy unique is the concept of tunable consistency. When a client writes or reads data, the engineer can specify how many replicas must acknowledge the request before it's considered successful. For example, you can choose to require all replicas (for stronger consistency) or just one replica (for higher availability) [101]. This flexibility allows Cassandra to adapt to different workloads and business requirements, while still maintaining fault tolerance across large clusters.
- Amazon Aurora's Six-Way Replication

  Amazon Aurora, part of AWS's managed relational database service, provides another strong example of replication in action. Aurora automatically replicates data across six copies, spread across three availability zones within a region. This ensures that even if multiple disks or an entire zone goes offline, the data is preserved and still accessible. Aurora also continuously backs up this data to Amazon S3, layering in additional durability [102], [103]. This design allows Aurora to promise much higher durability and availability compared to traditional databases, without engineers needing to configure complex replication setups themselves.

- Google Cloud Spanner and TrueTime

  Google Cloud's distributed database, Spanner takes replication one step further by combining it with a globally synchronized clock called TrueTime meaning that applications can use this clock to generate monotonically increasing time stamps so that any timestamp *T* is guaranteed to be greater than any other *T'* finished being generated before *T* started being generated [104]. Spanner replicates data across multiple regions and uses TrueTime to ensure strict consistency, even when replicas are thousands of miles apart. This allows Spanner to behave like a traditional relational database while still achieving global distribution. Spanner demonstrates that replication can solve not just fault tolerance problems, but also enable systems that scale across continents while preserving strong consistency guarantees.

- HDFS Block Replication

  The Hadoop Distributed File System (HDFS) is another classic example. When files are stored in HDFS, they are split into blocks and each block is replicated across multiple nodes (typically three). If one node fails, another node can serve the same data block, ensuring durability and availability [105]. This block-level replication model laid the groundwork for many distributed storage systems and is still foundational in big data ecosystems.

Consensus

Replication alone is not enough to guarantee that a distributed system will behave reliably. When multiple replicas exist across different nodes, the system needs a way to agree on which copy of the data is correct and which operations should be accepted. This is where consensus comes in. Consensus is the process of getting distributed nodes to agree on a single value or decision, even when some nodes fail, messages are delayed, or the network becomes unreliable.

At its core, consensus solves the "who do we trust?" problem. For example, if two clients try to update the same record at the same time, different replicas may temporarily store conflicting versions of the data. Without consensus, there is no clear way to determine which update should be accepted. Consensus algorithms ensure that all healthy nodes eventually agree on one consistent view of the data.

The most widely studied and implemented consensus protocols are Paxos and Raft. Paxos, proposed by Leslie Lamport, is theoretically elegant but notoriously complex to implement [106]. Raft was developed later as a more approachable alternative, designed with readability and practical deployment in mind [107]. Both algorithms work by requiring a majority of nodes (a quorum) to agree before an operation is committed. This way, even if some nodes fail or behave unpredictably, the system can still make progress and preserve correctness.

Consensus also explains some of the trade-offs in distributed systems. Achieving agreement among replicas introduces communication overhead and can reduce performance, especially across wide geographic distances. However, the benefit is consistency and reliability. Systems including etcd (used in Kubernetes), and Apache Zookeeper, all rely on consensus algorithms to coordinate distributed components. Consensus is the reason why cluster leaders can be elected, why metadata remains consistent across nodes, and why critical services can withstand failures without splitting into conflicting states.

Examples of Consensus in Action

- Raft in Kubernetes (etcd)

  Kubernetes, one of the most widely used orchestration platforms today, relies on consensus to manage its control plane. At the heart of Kubernetes is etcd, a distributed key-value store that uses the Raft consensus algorithm to maintain consistency across cluster states. When you create or update a resource (like a deployment or service), the information is written to etcd. Raft ensures that all members of the cluster agree on the new state before it's committed, even if some nodes crash [108]. Without consensus, Kubernetes clusters would quickly drift into inconsistent states, making workloads unreliable.
- Zookeeper in Hadoop and Kafka

  Apache Zookeeper is a system that is built around consensus. It was originally created to provide reliable coordination for Hadoop clusters, and it remains an important component for other distributed systems like Apache Kafka. Zookeeper ensures that services agree on things like leader election, configuration metadata, and membership of nodes. For instance, in Kafka, Zookeeper helps coordinate which broker is the controller and which partitions belong where. By ensuring cluster-wide agreement, Zookeeper prevents split-brain scenarios and keeps distributed services aligned [109].

Graceful Degradation

Even the most resilient distributed systems will encounter scenarios where part of the infrastructure fails, and full functionality cannot be maintained. The goal of graceful degradation is to design systems that continue to operate in a reduced but acceptable capacity rather than collapsing entirely. Instead of presenting users with downtime or errors, the system prioritizes critical functionality while limiting or disabling nonessential features until the issue is resolved.

A simple analogy is how modern cars behave when something goes wrong. If a tire loses air or the engine overheats, most cars can still operate in a limited "limp mode" that lets you safely reach a service station. Similarly, distributed systems designed with graceful degradation continue to provide essential services even under partial failure.

Graceful degradation can take many forms. In a data pipeline, if one enrichment service is unavailable, the system may still process records and mark missing values as null, ensuring that downstream analysis continues with slightly less detail rather than halting completely. In a recommendation system, if the machine learning model serving layer goes offline, the system might fall back to displaying top-selling or most popular items instead of personalized recommendations. Streaming systems like Flink may temporarily buffer events until downstream consumers recover, avoiding permanent data loss.

Graceful degradation is also closely tied to user experience. Users are often more tolerant of reduced features than outright downtime. For example, a cloud storage platform may disable advanced search temporarily but still allow uploads and downloads. This design philosophy keeps trust intact while giving engineers time to fix the underlying issue.

Implementing graceful degradation requires careful planning during system design. Engineers must identify critical services that must always remain operational and secondary services that can be disabled or limited. It also involves creating fallback mechanisms and clear monitoring to ensure that the degraded state is temporary, with recovery plans in place.

Self-Healing Systems

A key principle of modern fault tolerance is that systems after experiencing failure, should recover from them automatically. This is the idea behind self-healing systems. Instead of requiring human intervention for every issue, these systems detect failures, isolate the problem, and take corrective actions to restore functionality with little or no downtime.

At the core of self-healing systems is automation. Monitoring tools continuously track the health of nodes, processes, and services. When something goes wrong, automated responses are triggered. For example, if a server in a distributed cluster fails, orchestration platforms like Kubernetes automatically reschedule workloads on healthy nodes. If a pipeline job crashes, systems like Apache Airflow can retry tasks according to predefined rules, ensuring that transient issues do not derail the entire workflow.

Self-healing in modern systems can take place at multiple layers of the stack. At the infrastructure level, cloud providers are designed to handle hardware failures without manual intervention. If a server fails, the platform can automatically replace it and restore virtual machines from snapshots or replicas, ensuring that workloads continue to run with minimal disruption.

At the application level, self-healing is often built into microservices architectures. Techniques such as retry logic, circuit breakers, and automated health checks allow services to detect when a component is failing and reroute traffic away from it. This design maintains uptime while also helping the application adapt dynamically to transient failures.

Data systems also incorporate their own forms of self-healing. Distributed storage solutions mentioned before like HDFS and Amazon S3 automatically replicate missing blocks or files when a node goes down. By maintaining multiple copies across different nodes, these platforms guarantee durability and availability without requiring user intervention. Together, these layers of self-healing ensure that infrastructure, applications, and data remain resilient even in the face of failures.

One important aspect of self-healing is isolation. Systems must be designed so that failures do not cascade across the entire architecture. This might involve techniques like containerization, where each application runs in a sandboxed environment, or partitioning workloads so that a single failure affects only a subset of users.

Self-healing systems reduce operational overhead and allow teams to scale their infrastructure without proportionally increasing the need for manual maintenance. More importantly, they provide resilience against unpredictable issues, ensuring that business-critical services remain available.

Self-healing doesn't eliminate the need for human oversight. Engineers still need to monitor alerts, perform root cause analysis, and refine automated recovery rules. However, by embedding self-healing into system design, teams can minimize downtime and ensure that minor disruptions never become full-blown outages.

Real-World Architectures

All of the principles we've explored such as redundancy, replication, consensus, graceful degradation, and self-healing come together in real-world systems that power the technologies we use every day. Large-scale platforms do not rely on a single technique. Instead, they layer these strategies to create architectures that can survive failure at any level, whether it's a single disk, a server rack, or even an entire data center.

- Twitter's Manhattan

  Twitter's (now known as X) internal distributed storage system, called Manhattan, is built to serve billions of timeline updates, likes, retweets, and notifications in real time. Manhattan emphasizes low latency, global availability, and resilience under failure. It achieves this through sharding, replication across multiple data centers, and tunable consistency. By designing for redundancy at every layer, Manhattan ensures that no single data center outage can take down Twitter's core functionality, a key requirement for a platform where outages are highly visible to users worldwide [110].

- Alibaba's PolarDB

  Alibaba created PolarDB, a cloud-native relational database that is engineered to survive failures at scale. PolarDB replicates data across multiple availability zones and offers rapid failover when a node or zone becomes unavailable. Unlike traditional RDBMS systems, PolarDB uses a shared-storage architecture that separates compute from storage, allowing it to scale horizontally and recover quickly. Its design reflects the demands of e-commerce workloads like those seen during Black Friday, where fault tolerance and scalability are a must [111].

- Dropbox's Magic Pocket

  Dropbox's Magic Pocket is a custom-built storage system developed to replace their reliance on AWS S3. It was designed to handle hundreds of petabytes of data with redundancy, self-healing, and fault tolerance built into its architecture. Files are broken into blocks, replicated across different machines and data centers, and continuously verified for integrity. If corruption or loss is detected, missing blocks are rebuilt automatically [112]. Magic Pocket illustrates how a company can build a fault-tolerant distributed system tailored specifically to its business needs, with a focus on cost efficiency and durability.

Logging, Error Control, Debugging

Building a data pipeline that runs once is the easy part. Building one that runs every day, every hour, or in real time without breaking and costing the company revenue is much harder. Reliability is the true measure of a data engineer's craft, and three practices make reliability possible: logging, error control, and debugging.

Logs are the story your systems tell about what is happening under the hood. Error control ensures that when something goes wrong, it fails in a safe and predictable way instead of silently producing bad data. Debugging is the skill of finding and fixing problems quickly, a constant reality in any complex data environment.

Effective Logging

Logging is one of the most important practices for maintaining reliable data pipelines. At its core, logging means recording what your system is doing at any given point in time. Good logging is the difference between flying blind and having a clear picture of how and why a pipeline succeeded or failed. Logs serve as the narrative of your system. They capture events, provide context, and allow both humans and machines to interpret what has happened.

When building data pipelines, most engineers do not write logging functionality from scratch. Instead, they rely on logging libraries, which provide structured ways to record, format, and manage logs. A logging library is essentially a toolkit that abstracts away the tedious work of writing logs to files or consoles, handling log levels, and formatting messages. It allows engineers to focus on what to log, rather than how to store it.

In Python, the most common option is the built-in logging module. This library supports log levels, message formatting, and output to different destinations, known as "handlers." For example, you can configure logs to be written to a file for long-term storage, streamed to the console for real-time debugging, or sent directly to a centralized logging service. Because it's part of Python's standard library, it requires no extra setup and is widely used in ETL scripts [113].

Beyond the standard library, more specialized logging tools exist. Loguru is a popular Python package that simplifies logging by removing much of the boilerplate configuration, making it attractive for small teams or prototypes. In large-scale distributed environments, data engineers often extend these libraries with cloud-native logging tools. For instance, AWS CloudWatch, Google Cloud Logging, and Azure Monitor integrate tightly with their respective platforms and provide dashboards, search capabilities, and alerting built directly into the cloud ecosystem.

On the enterprise side, log aggregation systems like the ELK Stack, Splunk, or Datadog collect logs from multiple services and pipelines. These platforms let engineers filter logs by job ID, pipeline, or error type, and they support advanced features like alerting, visualization, and anomaly detection.

Logging libraries provide consistency. Instead of every developer writing logs in their own style, a library enforces standards in structure, severity, and destination. This consistency is critical

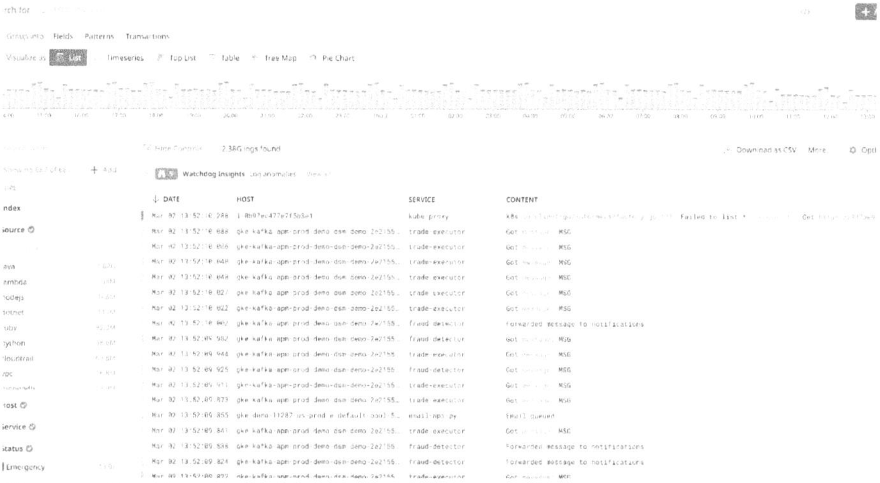

Figure 31: Datadog Logging [114]

when troubleshooting, where logs from extraction, transformation, and loading processes must all be pieced together to understand a failure.

When deciding what to log, how often to log, and what makes a log effective, it's important to think in terms of usefulness rather than volume. A good logging strategy records the flow of a pipeline from start to finish in a way that helps validate correctness, identify errors, and trace issues when they arise. That means capturing details such as job start and end times, the number of rows processed, schema validation results, performance metrics, and any errors or exceptions that occur. For batch processes, this often means logging at the beginning and end of each stage, with checkpoints for row counts or schema checks along the way. For streaming systems, where data flows continuously, logs should be more selective to avoid overwhelming the system, focusing on anomalies or checkpoints rather than every event.

What separates a good log from a poor one is clarity, context, and structure. A clear log is human-readable and easy to understand. Context ensures the message contains details like batch IDs, pipeline names, or error types that help pinpoint the issue quickly. Structured logs, often written in JSON or another consistent format, allow log management tools to parse and filter them easily. For ex-

```
{
  "timestamp": "2025-09-29T14:23:17Z",
  "level": "ERROR",
  "pipeline": "customer_ingestion_v2",
  "batch_id": "BATCH_20250929_1420",
  "step": "validation",
  "error_type": "NullValueError",
  "message": "Ingestion job failed due to null values in required field 'email_address'.",
  "record_count": 15432,
  "host": "ingest-node-3",
  "trace_id": "8f92c1e7-4a6d-4fa2-a87d-52a6a31a88d2"
}
```

Figure 32: A Strong Logging Message

ample, instead of simply stating "error occurred," a good log might specify that an ingestion job failed at the validation step due to null values in a required field, along with the batch ID and timestamp. This combination of precision and readability makes logs actionable, ensuring they serve as a reliable record rather than a noisy stream of text.

Effective Error Control

At its core, error control means designing your systems to fail in safe and predictable ways. Instead of crashing silently or producing bad data, a well-built pipeline surfaces errors clearly and prevents corrupted outputs from contaminating downstream systems. For example, if an extraction script cannot reach a database, error control mechanisms might retry the connection a set number of times with exponential backoff before logging a clear error and halting the job. This prevents false or partial data from slipping through. Similarly, transformation steps might enforce schema validation rules, automatically rejecting or quarantining bad records instead of letting them pollute the final dataset.

Error control is also about anticipation. Data engineers can use try/except blocks in Python, transaction rollbacks in SQL, or fault-tolerant design patterns in distributed systems to handle expected failure modes gracefully. Another common practice is to implement alerts tied to errors. When logs record an error event, some monitoring systems can automatically notify engineers, ensuring issues are caught quickly rather than days later when a stakeholder notices missing data in a dashboard.

The ultimate goal of error control is to make failures manageable. A well-controlled failure is one that doesn't break downstream systems, is logged with enough detail to diagnose, and is surfaced to the right people for resolution. This mindset shifts pipelines from being brittle to being resilient, which is essential when data workflows run continuously and at scale.

Debugging

Logging and error control help you capture when and where things go wrong. Debugging is the next step: figuring out why the problem happened and how to fix it. Debugging is not always straightforward because failures can come from many different layers. A bug might be in your own transformation code, in an upstream API, in the database schema, or in the orchestration system that schedules jobs. Unlike software debugging where you focus mainly on code, data engineering debugging often means untangling a mix of data issues and system issues at the same time.

The first principle of debugging is reproducibility. If you can reliably reproduce a failure, you can narrow down its cause. This might mean rerunning a pipeline with the same input data, isolating a problematic batch, or executing a single SQL transformation by hand. Structured logs and error handling make reproducibility possible by pointing you to the exact step and inputs that triggered the issue.

Once reproducibility is established, debugging involves tracing the flow of data through the system. A data engineer might check row counts after each stage to see where records dropped, validate schema changes to confirm alignment, or compare outputs against expected baselines. Debuggers also lean on their orchestration tools. Apache Airflow and Dagster allow engineers to rerun individual tasks or view task-level logs. Spark provides detailed stage and executor logs for tracing distributed jobs.

Debugging also benefits from using the right tools and strategies. Python scripts can be debugged with pdb or IDE debuggers, SQL queries can be tested interactively against smaller datasets, and distributed jobs can be tested locally with a subset of data before scaling to the full cluster. In practice, data engineers often build "sandbox" environments where they can replicate problems without disrupting production pipelines. Depending on your system, you might also use Postman to make mock API calls and verify that endpoints return the expected responses. By isolating API behavior in this way, you can catch integration issues early and reduce the time spent debugging larger workflows.

Debugging is both technical and investigative. It requires attention to detail, a methodical approach, and the ability to question assumptions about your code, your data, and even your infrastructure. Strong debugging practices reduce downtime, minimize wasted compute costs, and protect the integrity of downstream analytics. Being a strong debugger will make you a valuable asset to your organization, since you can demonstrate your technical ability and also your resilience in the face of complexity.

Emergencies and Disaster Recovery Plans

Even with all preventative measures, systems will fail due to factors outside of your control. Databases crash, pipelines break, servers go offline, and sometimes entire regions of a cloud provider become unavailable. These failures may be rare, but when they occur, they can have enormous consequences. Lost data, broken dashboards, or unavailable applications can cost organizations money and trust.

That is why resilience cannot rest only on prevention. Security measures reduce exposure to attacks, and fault tolerance helps systems withstand many common problems, but disaster recovery is what ensures that teams can respond when those safeguards aren't enough. It provides the structure for absorbing shocks, minimizing downtime, and restoring critical services.

Types of Emergencies

- Cyber Incidents

  Cyberattacks have become one of the most common threats to data systems. For example, in 2021, the Colonial Pipeline ransomware attack disrupted fuel supplies across the United States, showing how vulnerable critical infrastructure can be to cybercrime [115]. In a data engineering context, ransomware that encrypts pipeline servers or a denial-of-service attack against APIs could halt data flows for days.
- Data Breaches and Leaks

  A well-known example is the 2019 Capital One data breach, where a misconfigured cloud firewall allowed an attacker to access personal data of over 100 million customers [116]. This incident shows how a single error in cloud configuration can have massive consequences. Engineers working with APIs, cloud storage, or shared databases must ensure strict access controls and robust logging. Encryption and least-privilege policies help reduce the chance that an exposed system results in a full-scale data breach.
- System Failures

  In 2017, AWS S3 suffered an outage caused only by a simple command error during routine maintenance. For several hours, major websites and applications that relied on S3 were taken offline due to the domino effect of that simple command [117]. More recently, on October 20, 2025, AWS again suffered a large-scale outage, this time triggered by a DNS resolution failure in its Amazon DynamoDB endpoints in the US-East-1 region. That event cascaded across multiple services and applications worldwide, underscoring that even foundational cloud infrastructure is vulnerable. Although the failures were accidental, the broad reliance on AWS amplified its impact. This example demonstrates the importance of fault tolerance, redundancy, and testing recovery procedures, even when using trusted cloud providers.

- Natural Disasters

  In 2012, in addition to at least 117 deaths and over $50 billion dollars of damages, Hurricane Sandy also damaged data centers in New York and New Jersey, taking down services for days and causing physical destruction to hardware [118], [119]. Many organizations that had no disaster recovery plan struggled to restore operations. Today, multi-region replication and cloud infrastructure reduce this risk, but on-premises systems remain vulnerable. Engineers should always account for the possibility that an entire data center could become unavailable.

A Data Engineer's Disaster Recovery Plan

In the event of a catastrophe, a data engineer must have an immediate plan of action. The following steps listed will provide a rough outline, but it is important to tailor your disaster recovery plan within your individual context.

1. Immediate Triage

   The very first step in an emergency is triage. Just like doctors in an emergency ward, data engineers must quickly determine the scope and severity of the issue. This involves answering critical questions such as: Is essential data lost, corrupted, or merely delayed? Which services or pipelines are affected, and which stakeholders rely on them? What is the downstream impact on dashboards, analytics, or customer-facing applications?

   Triage also means distinguishing between symptoms and root causes. A broken dashboard might appear as the problem, but triage should uncover whether the failure lies in an upstream pipeline, a corrupt file, or a database outage. Effective triage is what prevents wasted time and directs engineers to the systems that matter most.

2. Communication and Coordination

   Crises do not unfold in silence. Communication during an

emergency is as important as technical response. Stakeholders want to know the current status, leadership needs clear expectations, and downstream users need reassurance about what to expect. Data engineers should set up a practice of providing frequent, transparent updates, even if the message is "we are still investigating." This reduces confusion and maintains trust.

Internal coordination is essential. Many organizations document escalation paths and incident response runbooks to avoid duplication of effort or contradictory fixes, all under a clear chain of command.

3. Containment

Containment means stopping the bleeding. Once the initial scope of the problem is understood, the priority is to prevent further damage. This might involve pausing ETL jobs to keep corrupted data from cascading into analytics warehouses, shutting off access to a compromised API, or routing data traffic away from a failing cluster.

Containment is not always about solving the problem, but about preserving options for recovery. Halting a pipeline quickly can preserve partial datasets that may still be valid, which can later be merged with restored data from backups. Similarly, freezing updates to a corrupted database ensures engineers can roll back to a consistent checkpoint without introducing further anomalies.

4. Recovery and Restoration

This stage is where backups and failover systems prove their worth. Recovery might involve restoring databases from nightly snapshots, replaying logs with point-in-time recovery, or rerunning pipelines from saved checkpoints. Hot backups allow for fast recovery with minimal downtime. Cold backups may take more time to restore but serve as insurance against catastrophic data loss.

Engineers may also lean on replication across regions, which allows failover to an unaffected data center. This was discussed in fault tolerance, but in practice it belongs here too: failing over from one region to another is often the fastest path to restore service.

5. Post-Mortem and Learning

   Once services are restored, the most valuable step begins: reflection. A post-mortem is conducted to answer: What exactly failed? How effective was triage, containment, and recovery? Did communication keep everyone aligned? Were backups sufficient, and did they restore data without unacceptable loss?

   These sessions are about improvement, not blame. Many teams adopt a blameless post-mortem culture so that engineers feel safe admitting mistakes. The focus should be on systemic fixes, such as improving automation, tightening documentation, or scheduling more frequent backups. For instance, if daily backups led to 12 hours of lost data, the lesson may be to introduce incremental backups every hour. If manual failover took too long, perhaps automation should handle the switchover.

Chapter 9

The Laws of Data Engineering

"Trust, but verify."

– Ronald Reagan [120]

Compliance and Regulation

Governmental compliance refers to the laws, regulations, and standards that govern how organizations collect, store, process, and share data. For data engineers, compliance is a legal obligation and an important factor in maintaining trust with clients, customers, and stakeholders. Understanding these requirements ensures that data handling practices meet both ethical and legal expectations.

Different regions and industries have their own specific rules. In the European Union, the General Data Protection Regulation (GDPR) sets strict guidelines for data privacy, consent, and the rights of individuals to access or delete their data. In the United States, the Health Insurance Portability and Accountability Act (HIPAA) governs how healthcare data is protected, while the Gramm-Leach-Bliley Act (GLBA) covers financial institutions. Other examples include the California Consumer Privacy Act (CCPA) and the Federal Information Security Management Act (FISMA) for federal agencies.

Compliance Generally

Compliance in data engineering begins with understanding that regulatory requirements aren't optional. They form a critical part of how data is stored, processed, and shared, regardless of the size of the organization or the specific technologies in use. At its core, compliance ensures that data handling aligns with established laws, industry standards, and ethical guidelines. These rules often dictate how long data can be kept, what kinds of data can be collected, and the security measures that must be in place to protect it.

One of the first steps in meeting compliance obligations is identifying the type of data being handled. PII, financial records, and health data all have their own unique rules and associated protections. Misclassifying data can lead to gaps in security and unintended breaches of compliance. Imagine treating healthcare data as if it were general customer contact information. The difference in care/importance can very easily result in violations of privacy laws. Data classification frameworks help ensure that every dataset is properly tagged and managed according to its sensitivity and regulatory category.

Another important consideration is data lifecycle management. Regulations often extend beyond how data is stored to cover its entire lifespan, from initial collection to eventual deletion. Compliance policies should define how data is ingested, secured, accessed, and disposed of, with clear documentation of each step. This includes understanding retention periods required by law and having automated systems in place to delete or anonymize data when those periods expire.

Compliance also requires that technical and organizational measures are integrated into the architecture from the start rather than added after systems are built. This approach, often referred to as "compliance by design," ensures that the necessary controls (we will cover security later) such as encryption, access permissions, and audit logging are an inherent part of data systems. It also reduces the risk and cost of retrofitting compliance measures as laws and policies inevitably evolve.

Compliance Across the United States

Within the U.S., compliance requirements vary widely between federal and state.

At the federal level, compliance is often framed around broad privacy and consumer protection mandates. The Federal Trade Commission (FTC) enforces standards against unfair or deceptive practices, which extends to how organizations collect, store, and share personal information. Other federal rules establish requirements for data security, breach notification, and transparency in handling personal data, ensuring that organizations maintain accountability at a national level. These provide a baseline of protection, even as more detailed obligations are layered on at the state level.

At the state level, privacy laws have become increasingly influential. The California Consumer Privacy Act (CCPA) and its amendment, the California Privacy Rights Act (CPRA), impose strict requirements for consumer data privacy, including rights to access, delete, and opt out of the sale of personal information [121]. Other states, such as Virginia (VCDPA) and Colorado (CPA), have implemented similar laws, each with its own definitions, enforcement mechanisms, and exemptions [122], [123]. A data engineer working for a nationwide organization must account for these differences to ensure that systems and processes remain compliant across jurisdictions.

To meet these regional demands, U.S.-based data engineers often build systems capable of tagging and classifying data at ingestion, enforcing retention policies, and applying access controls based on jurisdiction. Automated workflows that adjust for state-specific requirements can greatly reduce operational complexity and the risk of violations. Documentation of these processes is equally important, as regulators may require evidence of compliance during audits.

Designing systems with adaptability in mind ensures that they can handle the evolving and often fragmented landscape of U.S. data regulations. This approach also sets a foundation for expanding compliance efforts to meet international standards.

Compliance Internationally

When operating outside the United States, organizations face an even more complex compliance environment. Each country or region enforces its own legal frameworks, often with stricter requirements than U.S. laws. A prime example is the European Union's General Data Protection Regulation (GDPR), which has become a global benchmark for privacy standards. GDPR applies not only to businesses operating within the EU, but also to any organization that processes the personal data of EU residents, regardless of where the organization is located. This means a U.S.-based company with international customers must still comply with GDPR's rules on consent, data minimization, breach notification, and the "right to be forgotten [124]."

Other countries have developed their own privacy and data

protection laws that may differ in scope and enforcement. Canada's Personal Information Protection and Electronic Documents Act (PIPEDA), Brazil's Lei Geral de Proteção de Dados (LGPD), Australia's Privacy Act, and Singapore's Personal Data Protection Act (PDPA) each carry unique obligations [125], [126], [127], [128]. Some laws focus more heavily on cross-border data transfers, requiring organizations to store certain data locally or prove adequate safeguards before moving it abroad.

Cultural differences can also shape compliance strategies. In some regions, data privacy is viewed primarily as a legal obligation, while in others it's considered a fundamental human right. These perspectives influence how laws are written, interpreted, and enforced. Data engineers working in global contexts must therefore understand the letter of the law and its intent and local expectations.

The most effective international compliance programs rely on clear documentation of data flows, consistent classification of personal data, and technical controls that can adapt to different legal frameworks. This often means working closely with legal and compliance teams to maintain a live map of applicable regulations. Organizations that succeed in international compliance treat it as an ongoing process rather than a one-time setup, continuously adjusting to new laws and evolving interpretations.

Compliance Across Sector and Industry

Compliance requirements can differ significantly depending on the industry in which an organization operates. Different sectors handle different categories of sensitive data, and laws or standards are tailored to address the unique risks in each domain. For example, healthcare organizations in the United States must comply with the HIPAA, which governs the protection and secure transmission of patient health information. The Health Insurance Portability and Accountability Act (HIPAA) enforces strict safeguards around data storage, sharing, and breach reporting only in organizations that deal with sensitive health records [129].

In the financial sector, regulations such as the Gramm-Leach-Bliley Act (GLBA) and Payment Card Industry Data Security Standard (PCI DSS) establish rules for safeguarding customer financial data, protecting against fraud, and securing payment systems. These requirements may include encryption standards, regular security testing, and limitations on how long certain data can be stored [130]. Similarly, publicly traded companies are subject to the Sarbanes-Oxley Act (SOX), which mandates specific internal controls and auditing processes to ensure the integrity of financial reporting [131].

Even in industries that are not as heavily regulated, there are often voluntary frameworks and certifications that organizations adopt to demonstrate a commitment to security and data protection. Examples include the International Organization for Standardization's ISO/IEC 27001 standard for information security management and the Center for Internet Security's CIS Controls. Adopting these standards can help an organization stand out in competitive markets, strengthen trust with customers, and prepare for potential future regulations.

Understanding industry-specific requirements is essential because these rules often dictate technical implementation choices. The type of data collected, the retention period, the encryption methods, and even the architecture of storage systems may be shaped by compliance demands. Through working closely with compliance teams, data engineers can ensure that pipelines, databases, and analytics platforms meet not just technical performance goals, but also the legal and ethical obligations of their industry.

Chapter 10

Fortifying Data Infrastructures

"Security is a process, not a product."

– Bruce Schneier[132]

Cybersecurity for Data Engineers

Security is not just the responsibility of specialized cybersecurity teams. Whether handling customer records, financial transactions, or proprietary business metrics, you're a steward of sensitive information. This means security must be embedded in every stage of your work, from data ingestion to storage to analysis.

Unauthorized access, data breaches, and system exploits are persistent risks in the increasingly complex threat landscape. A single vulnerability in a pipeline or database can lead to stolen data, regulatory fines, or irreparable damage to an organization's reputation. With consideration to the evolving privacy regulations and industry specific compliance issues that we covered in the previous chapter, data engineers have to design systems that meet both technical and legal requirements for protecting data.

Security Frameworks

Before diving into the specific tools and techniques a data engineer can use to secure data, it's important to ground ourselves in the principles that guide these decisions. One of the most widely recognized is the CIA Triad: Confidentiality, Integrity, and Availability. This simple but powerful model serves as the backbone for nearly every security strategy, and it's just as relevant for managing a data pipeline as it's for securing a corporate network.

Confidentiality is the principle of keeping data private and preventing unauthorized access. In a data engineering context, this can mean encrypting data in transit and at rest, securing API keys in a secrets manager, and enforcing strict access controls on databases and storage systems.

Integrity ensures that the data collected and processed remains accurate and uncorrupted. Techniques such as hashing, checksums, and digital signatures can help detect unauthorized modifications. Version control for datasets and clear data lineage tracking are also important for maintaining integrity in complex pipelines.

Availability is about making sure that data remains accessible to the people and systems that need it when they need it. This can involve building fault-tolerant infrastructure, implementing database replication, or designing failover strategies for critical services. Availability often means balancing performance with redundancy so that analytics, machine learning models, and operational systems remain functional at all times [133].

Understanding and applying the CIA Triad in a data engineering workflow helps ensure that a pipeline is both secure and dependable. From here, we will explore specific tools and techniques such as encryption, secure tunnels, and layered access controls that support these principles in practice.

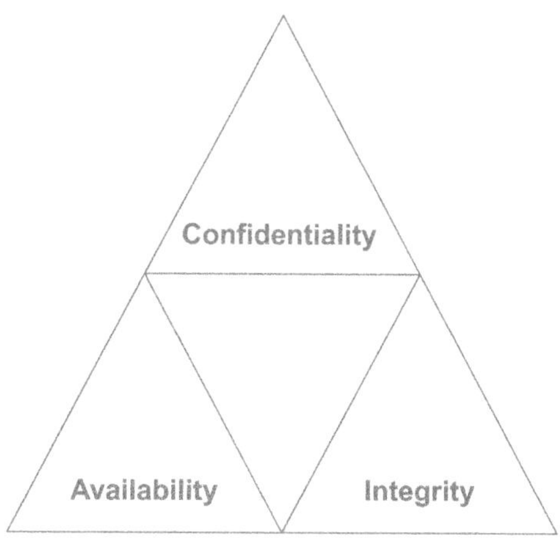

Figure 33: The CIA Triad

Encryption

Encryption is the process of converting readable information–known as plaintext–into an unreadable format–called ciphertext–using an algorithm and a key. Only someone with the correct key can reverse the process and turn the ciphertext back into its original form, a step known as decryption. This ensures that even if data is intercepted or stolen, it remains unusable to anyone without authorized access. Encryption is the primary method for protecting sensitive information, especially when handling customer records, financial trans actions, intellectual property, or regulated datasets. It's typically applied in two main contexts: in transit and at rest.

Encryption in transit safeguards data while it's moving between systems. Common implementations include transport layer security (TLS) for securing API calls, Hypertext Transfer Protocol Secure (HTTPS) for encrypting web requests, and Secure Shell (SSH) tunnels for secure remote connections. For example, streaming IoT data to a cloud warehouse should always involve encryption to prevent anyone monitoring the network from viewing the raw values.

Encryption at rest protects data stored on disk or in a database. This might mean enabling native encryption in a database like PostgreSQL, configuring server-side encryption for cloud storage or encrypting entire volumes using services like AWS EBS encryption. For compliance-heavy scenarios, a dedicated Key Management Service (KMS) or Hardware Security Module (HSM) is often used to securely generate, store, and rotate encryption keys.

Secure Tunnels

A secure tunnel is an encrypted pathway that allows data to travel safely between two endpoints over an otherwise insecure network such as the public internet. You can think of it as sending a sealed, tamper-proof package through a delivery service. The package may pass through many hands, but the contents remain hidden and intact until it reaches the intended recipient.

Secure tunnels are especially useful when systems that handle sensitive information need to communicate across environments

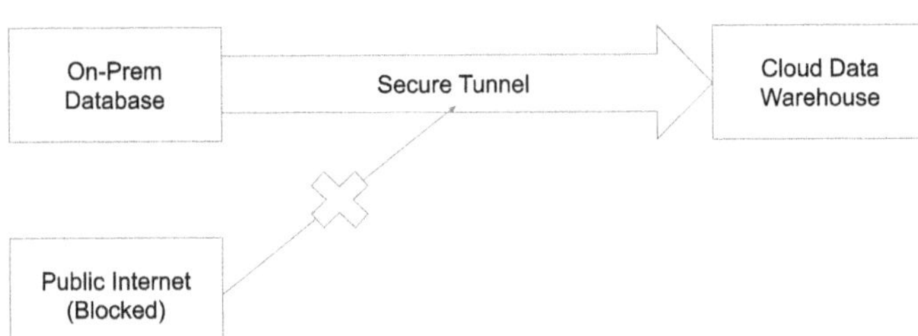

Figure 34: A Simple Secure Tunnel

that are fully trusted. One common example is an SSH tunnel, which securely forwards ports between local and remote machines. This method is often used to access databases or internal services without exposing them directly to the internet. Another example is a Virtual Private Network (VPN), which creates an encrypted connection between remote locations, allowing developers or data pipelines to access private network resources from anywhere. In cloud environments, services such as AWS Direct Connect, Azure ExpressRoute, and Google Cloud Interconnect provide dedicated, secure links between on-premises data centers and cloud infrastructure.

Using secure tunnels ensures that the data is encrypted in transit and that the communication channel itself is authenticated and protected from unauthorized access. This approach is important for pipelines that pull or push data to multiple environments, such as staging and production systems, or when transferring information between different geographic regions.

When secure tunnels are combined with strong encryption and robust identity management, the risk of interception, tampering, or exposure of sensitive information during transfer is significantly reduced. This makes them an essential tool in the security toolkit of a modern data engineer.

Access Control and the Principle of Least Privilege

Access control is the practice of ensuring that only authorized users, systems, or processes can access specific data or resources. While encryption protects the contents of data and secure tunnels protect it during transit, access control determines who is allowed to see or use that data in the first place.

A key concept in access control is the Principle of Least Privilege (PoLP). This principle means that each user, service account, or process should have the minimum level of access necessary to perform its job and nothing more. For example, if an ETL service only needs to read data from a source system and write it to a warehouse, it should not have permissions to delete records or access unrelated systems. Limiting privileges in this way reduces the risk of accidental damage and minimizes the potential impact if an account is compromised.

Access control is enforced through two main processes: authentication and authorization. Authentication verifies the identity of the user or system, using methods such as passwords, API keys, multi-factor authentication (MFA), or certificates. Authorization then determines what that authenticated identity is allowed to do. Role-based access control (RBAC) assigns permissions based on job roles, while attribute-based access control (ABAC) uses attributes such as department, location, or project.

Access control often spans multiple environments, from cloud platforms and databases to version control systems and orchestration tools. Consistent application of the PoLP across all these systems is critical to maintaining a secure data ecosystem.

Access control should not be a one-time configuration. Permissions need to be reviewed regularly, especially when roles change or projects end. Combining access control with strong encryption and secure tunnels creates a layered defense that protects data from both unauthorized access and accidental exposure.

Auditing and Monitoring

Even with strong encryption, secure tunnels, and strict access control, no security system is perfect. Threats can still arise from misconfigurations, insider actions, or unknown vulnerabilities.

Auditing involves reviewing system activity and configurations to ensure that security policies are being followed. This might include checking database access logs, reviewing cloud IAM permissions, or confirming that encryption settings are properly enabled. Regular audits can help identify potential weaknesses before they become problems. For example, an audit might reveal that a service account has unused write permissions, which can then be removed to reduce risk.

Monitoring focuses on continuously observing systems for unusual or suspicious activity. This can involve real-time alerts for failed login attempts, large data exports, or changes to critical system configurations. Many organizations use Security Information and Event Management (SIEM) systems to collect and analyze log data from across the infrastructure. Think setting up automated alerts when unexpected queries run against a production database or large amounts of data leaving a secure network.

Auditing and monitoring work best together. Audits provide a structured, periodic check to verify compliance and configuration integrity, while monitoring offers ongoing visibility and the ability to respond quickly to incidents. Both functions should be documented, and findings should be integrated into a continuous improvement process so that the security posture evolves alongside the data environment.

Insecure APIs and Endpoints

APIs, as we've touched upon, are a core part of modern data engineering workflows. They power ETL processes, feed analytics pipelines, and serve as integration points between internal and external systems. However, poorly secured APIs can be a significant vulnerability that exposes sensitive data or allows unauthorized access to critical systems.

One of the most common issues is the absence or weakness of authentication. An API that doesn't require credentials or relies on static keys embedded in code can easily be exploited. Even if authentication is present, improper implementation such as sending credentials over unencrypted channels can put data at risk. Using strong authentication mechanisms like OAuth 2.0 or signed requests in the APIs you work with is key and that secrets are stored securely rather than hard-coded into scripts.

Rate limiting is another crucial consideration. Without it, a malicious actor could flood an endpoint with requests, leading to denial-of-service attacks or excessive costs in pay-per-request systems. Data engineers also need to be aware of excessive data exposure, where an API returns far more information than necessary. For example, a customer lookup endpoint might return entire records including addresses, phone numbers, and payment details, even when only an ID or name is needed.

To mitigate these risks, collaborate with development and security teams to ensure API designs follow security best practices. This includes enforcing authentication and authorization, validating and sanitizing inputs, limiting response fields, and transmitting data over HTTPS. Tools like Postman can help with manual testing, while security scanners such as OWASP ZAP can identify vulnerabilities during automated checks.

APIs are only as secure as their weakest implementation detail. A single exposed endpoint can compromise the security of an entire data platform. It's critical to understand both how to use APIs securely and how to identify signs that one may be at risk.

Credential Management

The most common and risky secrets in a data platform are the straightforward ones—API keys, database passwords, OAuth client secrets, and access tokens. They need the same planning and care you give to schemas and pipelines. Store them in a central secrets manager backed by key management, fetch them at runtime through a trusted mechanism, and tie every retrieval to a real identity so you can see who accessed what, from where, and when. This keeps plaintext credentials out of repos and images, reduces the impact of a leak, and provides a single place to enforce policy and review activity.

Risk often comes from scope and lifetime. Issue separate credentials per workload and environment, grant only the actions the task requires, and, where supported, bind usage to context—service identities, mutual TLS, private connectivity, or IP ranges—so a copied key is hard to use elsewhere. Favor short-lived tokens minted on demand over long-lived keys, and design pipelines to refresh tokens automatically without manual steps or downtime.

Treat credentials as managed objects with a clear lifecycle. Define how they are created, distributed, renewed, revoked, and retired. Automate rotation on a regular cadence and use overlap windows so old and new values run in parallel while you verify behavior before cutover. Rotate on role changes, vendor advisories, and scope updates, and remove unused secrets quickly, since anything sitting unmonitored tends to surface at the worst time.

Smooth workflows help people do the right thing. Provide a standard path where jobs receive secrets at runtime and code references a stable handle rather than a literal value. Mask secrets in logs and telemetry. Add secret scanning to pre-commit and CI to catch accidental inclusion before merge. Offer sandbox credentials with narrow scope and synthetic data for local work to reduce the pull toward production keys.

Visibility and response complete the picture. Monitor for unusual reads from the vault, authentications from new regions or networks, and sudden spikes of activity tied to a single key. Keep clean audit trails so you can reconstruct events. Rehearse the steps for suspected exposure—revoke affected values in order, invalidate active sessions, tighten network reachability, and notify downstream owners with clear guidance. Handled this way, API keys and passwords become observable, time-boxed dependencies rather than silent liabilities, and the platform remains resilient even when an individual secret fails.

Other Frameworks and Considerations

While the CIA Triad provides a strong foundation, it isn't the only security framework worth knowing. Models like Zero Trust Architecture (ZTA) emphasize confidentiality by assuming that no user or system should be trusted by default, even inside your network [134]. Standards like NIST Cybersecurity Framework and ISO/IEC 27001 give structured approaches for identifying, protecting, detecting, responding to, and recovering from security incidents [135], [136]. By understanding these guiding frameworks, data engineers can better evaluate the security posture of their systems and select the right measures to protect data at every stage of the pipeline.

Chapter 11

Intro to Data Governance

"You can have data without information, but you cannot have information without data."

- Daniel Keys Moran [137]

Governing your Data

It should be obvious to you now that data is the most valuable asset any organization holds, but getting the most out of it depends on how well it's managed, protected, and made available to those who need it. This is where data governance comes in. At its core, data governance is the framework of policies, processes, and responsibilities that ensures data is accurate, secure, consistent, and used responsibly across the organization.

Governance provides the guardrails that shape how pipelines are designed, how data is stored, and how access is controlled. Effective data governance is what allows data to be trusted by analysts, data scientists, executives, and even customers. Without it, organizations risk decisions being made on bad data, security vulnerabilities being overlooked, and compliance gaps exposing them to legal consequences.

This chapter will explore the key elements of data governance, including data quality management, data ownership and stewardship, access control, compliance requirements, metadata management, and monitoring. We'll also discuss how governance differs from but complements security, and how engineers play a central role in translating governance policies into technical practices. Governance is not red tape, but an enabler of reliable, secure, and scalable data systems.

Data Quality Management

High-quality data is the foundation of every trustworthy data system. Even with sophisticated pipelines, analytics, or machine learning models, they are only as reliable as the data they run on. Data quality management (DQM) is the set of practices and processes that ensures data is accurate, complete, consistent, and reliable for use across the organization.

Dimensions of Data Quality

Data engineers often evaluate data quality through several key dimensions that together provide a framework for assessing overall health. Accuracy ensures the data reflects reality, since even small mistakes like an incorrect customer address can undermine advanced systems. Completeness asks whether all necessary values are present, as missing fields in a sales record can distort revenue projections. Consistency focuses on whether data matches across systems, because if finance shows one total while sales shows another, trust is lost. Timeliness addresses whether data is up to date, since stale shipment information frustrates customers and disrupts operations. Validity checks whether values conform to expected formats or rules, such as rejecting an impossible date like "31/02/2024." Finally, uniqueness ensures records are not duplicated, since multiple entries for the same customer can inflate counts and mislead analysis. By monitoring these dimensions together, data engineers gain a clear, structured way to measure and maintain the reliability of their datasets.

To maintain data quality, engineers apply a range of technical practices, many of which you have already seen in earlier discussions. Validation rules ensure incoming data meets constraints by checking required fields, ranges, or formats before records are accepted. Deduplication routines help identify and merge duplicate entries across systems, reducing noise and improving accuracy. Automated profiling tools scan datasets to flag anomalies or outliers, while monitoring frameworks send alerts if there are sudden changes in data volume, distribution, or schema. Lineage tracking adds another layer of control by capturing how data moves and transforms across pipelines, making it easier to trace errors back to their source. Modern tools such as Great Expectations, Monte Carlo, and dbt tests help automate these tasks, allowing teams to detect and address issues early before they reach end users.

Why It Matters for Governance

Employing data governance practices without data quality is like a library with mislabeled books: you may have a cataloging system, but the information is not usable or trustworthy. For governance policies to work, the underlying data must be accurate and dependable. Poor data quality undermines compliance, erodes business trust, and forces teams to waste time fixing problems downstream instead of focusing on higher-value tasks.

Owning data quality means building checks and balances directly into pipelines, documenting assumptions about data, and ensuring that issues are surfaced early. It is not glamorous work, but it is essential for making governance real.

Examples of poor versus strong data quality can be seen clearly in industries like e-commerce and financial services. For an online retailer, customer records are often stored across several systems. In a poorly managed environment, the same customer might appear multiple times, such as "Jon Smith," "Jonathan Smith," or even "Jhn Smith," each tied to a different email or address. When marketing runs a campaign, this results in duplicate messages, wasted spend, and an annoyed customer. With strong data quality practices such as deduplication and validation, however, the retailer ensures each individual is represented by a single, accurate record, leading to targeted campaigns, lower costs, and a better customer experience. A similar contrast arises in financial reporting. A bank may pull transaction data from multiple systems to prepare quarterly statements. If one system records transactions in local currency and another in U.S. dollars without flagging the difference, the combined report could overstate or understate totals. This inconsistency risks poor decisions or even compliance violations. With robust governance and clear metadata management, data engineers can enforce consistent tracking of currency types, preserving both accuracy and regulatory compliance.

Data Ownership and Stewardship

One of the biggest challenges in any organization is figuring out who's responsible for data. When something goes wrong, whether it's a data quality issue, a compliance failure, or a broken pipeline, confusion over ownership can delay fixes and create finger-pointing. Data governance addresses this problem by clearly defining data ownership and data stewardship.

Data ownership means assigning ultimate responsibility for specific datasets to individuals or teams. A data owner is accountable for how data is collected, stored, secured, and used. They make decisions about access rights, retention policies, and quality standards. For example, in a university, the registrar's office might own student enrollment data, while the finance office owns billing data.

Ownership provides a clear point of accountability, which is essential for ensuring compliance and building trust in data systems. Without ownership, datasets can become "orphaned," where no one feels responsible for their accuracy or maintenance.

While owners set the rules, data stewards carry out the daily work of ensuring those rules are followed. Stewards are often data engineers, analysts, or business users who maintain data quality, monitor metadata, and ensure compliance policies are applied in practice. For instance, a data steward might notice missing values in a dataset and flag the issue for correction, or ensure that a data catalog is kept up to date so that others can discover and use the data properly.

Stewardship emphasizes that governance is not just theoretical and that it is lived out in day-to-day workflows. Effective stewardship ensures that data policies are not just written down but actively practiced.

Clear ownership and stewardship prevent confusion, reduce redundancy, and strengthen compliance. They ensure accountability while also building a culture where data is treated as an organizational asset rather than a byproduct. In regulated industries, being able to point to an accountable owner can be the difference between passing and failing an audit.

Data Catalogs and Discoverability

As organizations expand, the number of datasets, pipelines, and storage systems often grows even faster. Without proper organization, this creates a major challenge: people know the data exists, but they cannot find it or do not know whether they can trust it. An organization can be said to have poor discoverability if its data is disorganized in this way. Poor discoverability leads to the rise of "shadow data," where teams keep their own spreadsheets or rogue databases because they cannot access the official data. A well-maintained data catalog solves this problem by acting as a central inventory of all available data assets thereby increasing discoverability.

A modern data catalog goes well beyond simply listing datasets. It provides rich metadata, including schema details, data types, lineage, and usage statistics, giving teams a clear understanding of how data is structured and where it comes from. It also highlights ownership and stewardship information, so users know who is accountable for maintaining each dataset.

Quality indicators are another key feature, showing when the data was last updated, whether it passed validation checks, and how complete it is. On top of that, a catalog offers powerful search and discovery capabilities, enabling analysts, engineers, and business users to quickly find the right dataset without needing to rely on IT or data engineering teams for guidance.

For instance, finance teams can rely on a catalog to quickly identify the official source of revenue data, avoiding the confusion of multiple conflicting spreadsheets. Data scientists can use it to discover existing customer churn datasets, saving time that would otherwise be spent preparing raw data. Meanwhile, data engineers benefit from catalog lineage tools, which allow them to trace how one dataset depends on another and anticipate downstream impacts before making schema changes.

Tools for Data Catalogs

Several modern platforms provide catalog and discoverability features. Open-source options include Amundsen (by Lyft) and DataHub (by LinkedIn). Commercial tools like Collibra, Alation, and Informatica provide richer governance workflows and integrations with compliance frameworks. Many cloud platforms, such as AWS Glue Data Catalog, Google Data Catalog, and Azure Purview, also offer integrated catalogs that link directly with their storage and pipeline services.

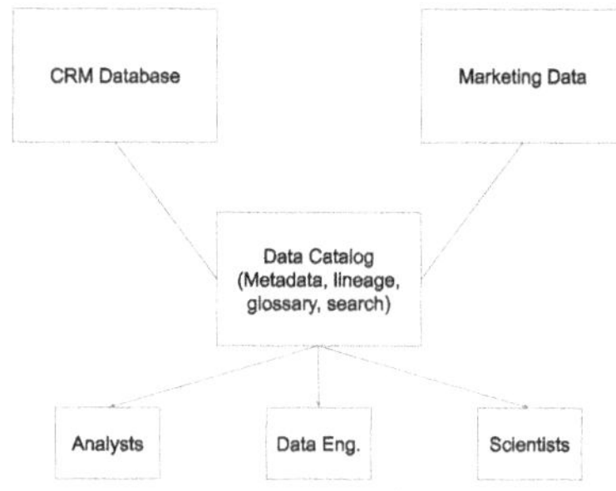

Figure 35: A Simple Data Catalog

Master Data Management

As organizations grow, they often end up with multiple systems that hold overlapping or conflicting versions of the same core data. A customer might appear in the CRM, the billing system, the marketing database, and the support ticket platform, each with slightly different details. This fragmentation creates serious challenges for data quality, consistency, and trust. Master Data Management is the discipline that addresses this problem by creating a "single version of the truth" for the most important data entities.

What is Master Data?

While a data catalog helps people discover and understand what data exists, MDM ensures that the data itself is accurate, consistent, and trustworthy across systems. Master data refers to the key business entities that are used across systems and processes. Common examples include customers, with details such as names, addresses, and account numbers; products, with information like SKUs, descriptions, categories, and pricing; employees, with identifiers, departments, and roles; and vendors or partners. Unlike transactional data which captures individual events like purchases or website clicks, master data remains relatively stable over time. It provides the reference framework that transactional data depends on, acting as a consistent foundation across the organization.

Master Data Management (MDM) solutions bring order to these critical entities by consolidating them into a central hub or "golden record." This process usually begins with ingestion, where data about entities is pulled in from multiple source systems. Next comes matching and deduplication, where the solution identifies when multiple records actually refer to the same entity. Once duplicates are resolved, merging occurs, creating a single unified record that combines the most accurate or authoritative attributes from each source. Finally, this golden record is distributed back to systems or made accessible through APIs, ensuring consistency everywhere it's needed.

The presence or absence of MDM has a major impact on daily work. Without it, engineers spend enormous amounts of time reconciling inconsistencies across systems, which slows down pipelines, introduces errors into analytics, and undermines trust in reporting. With MDM in place, analysts and data scientists can work confidently with standardized, reliable entity data. It also simplifies compliance requirements such as meeting GDPR's "right to be forgotten" since customer data can be centrally tracked and updated. On the operational side, systems function more smoothly because every application references the same authoritative source of truth for entities like customers, products, or employees.

There are dedicated MDM platforms such as Informatica MDM, Talend Data Fabric, and IBM InfoSphere, which provide full-featured governance and synchronization capabilities. Cloud providers also offer integrated solutions, such as AWS Glue DataBrew for preparation. In smaller organizations, simpler tools like dbt transformations combined with data catalogs can approximate MDM by enforcing consistent definitions and cleaning entity records.

Data Lineage and Provenance

Even in well-governed environments, one of the most common questions stakeholders ask is: "Where did this data come from, and how has it changed?" That is where data lineage and provenance come into play. These concepts provide transparency, trust, and accountability across the data lifecycle.

What is Data Lineage?

Data lineage describes the full lifecycle of data as it moves through a system. It tracks data from its origin (such as an API, RDBMS, or flat file), through each transformation and pipeline stage, to its final resting place in a warehouse, data lake, or report. Lineage is essential for debugging issues and for ensuring compliance. If someone reports a problem in a KPI, being able to trace its lineage lets engineers quickly find whether the root cause lies in a source system, a transformation step, or a modeling error. This is where your data flow diagrams can be a tremendous source of reference.

What is Data Provenance?

Data provenance is closely related, but slightly different. Provenance is the historical record of where data originated and what happened to it over time. While lineage focuses on the flow of data through systems, provenance provides a deeper audit trail. It can include metadata like who modified the data, which scripts or pipelines were used, when transformations occurred, and what versions of the data exist.

For example, in scientific research, provenance ensures that a dataset used for analysis is reproducible: it shows not just the current version of the dataset but also the exact steps and environments that led to it. In business, provenance is often used in compliance contexts to prove that sensitive data has been handled correctly and not tampered with.

Why Lineage and Provenance Matter

Lineage and provenance play a critical role in strengthening data governance. They provide transparency by showing stakeholders exactly how numbers in a report were produced, increasing trust in the outputs. They also establish accountability, allowing data owners and stewards to trace errors or inconsistencies back to their source. From a compliance standpoint, regulators often require proof of data handling practices, and lineage or provenance records serve as the evidence needed to demonstrate proper controls. Finally, these practices improve efficiency for engineers, who can save significant time troubleshooting issues when they have visibility into the full path and history of data.

Chapter 12
Trade-offs in Data Systems

"There is no silver bullet."

– Fred Brooks [138]

No Free Lunch

One of the biggest differences between a novice and a production-grade data pipeline is in how well it works. Building a system that delivers data from point A to point B is an achievement, but in the fast-paced world of modern organizations, efficiency is just as important as functionality. A pipeline that runs slowly, costs too much to operate, or requires constant babysitting quickly becomes a liability rather than an asset. That is why optimization is not be treated as an afterthought for data engineers and should be part of the very foundation of professional practice.

Optimization in data engineering goes beyond making things "faster." We must carefully tune systems so that they perform reliably at scale, remain cost-effective, and don't consume unnecessary resources. A poorly written query that runs in minutes today could take hours when the dataset grows tenfold. An oversized cluster may process jobs quickly, but it might also double the monthly cloud bill. And a lack of automation might force engineers to spend their time fighting fires instead of building new capabilities. The ability to optimize systems ensures that data engineers can balance these competing needs while delivering dependable pipelines that meet business demands.

As organizations increasingly rely on real-time dashboards, machine learning models, and large-scale analytics, the pressure to optimize has never been higher. Executives want fast insights without runaway infrastructure costs. Analysts want quick query responses without waiting for overnight jobs. Data scientists want clean, accessible data without delays. Meeting all these demands requires a systematic approach to optimization, one that balances performance, cost, and operational efficiency.

Performance Optimization

Performance optimization in data engineering is about ensuring that pipelines and systems can handle increasing data volumes and user demands without grinding to a halt. It's not just about speed for its own sake. Well-optimized systems improve reliability, reduce costs indirectly, and allow organizations to scale without constant rework. Below are the core techniques and practices that data engineers use to optimize performance.

Many performance bottlenecks in data systems originate from poorly written queries. SQL, in particular, offers developers tremendous flexibility, but that same flexibility means there are often multiple ways to write the same query—some far less efficient than others. For this reason, data engineers must be able to analyze query execution plans, minimize full table scans, and ensure that indexing strategies are correctly applied.

Optimizations can be both simple and highly impactful. For instance, replacing SELECT * with explicit column names prevents the transfer of unnecessary data. Similarly, using window functions judiciously can outperform deeply nested subqueries, reducing computational overhead. Partitioning large tables by date, category, or another logical key further improves performance by ensuring queries scan only the relevant slices of data instead of the entire dataset. Even seemingly modest improvements in query structure or indexing can compound at scale, leading to exponential time savings and more responsive systems.

```
Inefficient: pulls all columns, even unused ones
SELECT *
FROM sales
WHERE sale_date >= '2023-01-01';

Optimized: only retrieves columns needed for analysis
SELECT sale_id, customer_id, sale_date, total_amount
FROM sales
WHERE sale_date >= '2023-01-01';
```

Figure 36: Unoptimized vs. Optimized SQL Query

Caching Strategies

Caching is another powerful optimization technique that can dramatically improve performance. By temporarily storing frequently accessed results, caching reduces the need to reprocess the same data repeatedly, saving both time and computing resources. This is especially useful in environments where certain queries or reports are run frequently with the same parameters.

There are several common approaches to caching. In relational databases, materialized views allow pre-computed results to be stored and refreshed on a schedule, speeding up queries that would otherwise require expensive joins or aggregations. In-memory caching tools such as Redis or Memcached store query outputs in fast, volatile memory, making them ideal for high-throughput applications where responsiveness is critical. Many modern cloud warehouses, including Snowflake and BigQuery, provide built-in query result caching, automatically reusing results when the underlying data has not changed.

Scheduling and Workload Management

Not all data jobs need to run simultaneously, and performance often degrades when too many resource-heavy tasks compete at once. Careful scheduling spreads workloads more evenly, avoids peak contention, and keeps pipelines responsive. Running batch jobs during low-traffic windows and ensuring critical processes have priority are simple ways to boost throughput and reduce unnecessary delays.

While we've already touched on orchestration, it's worth noting that these platforms give data engineers the fine-grained control needed to tune performance at scale. Adjusting task concurrency, staggering job start times, or defining dependencies more precisely can make a noticeable difference in how smoothly pipelines run. Even small improvements in orchestration can prevent cascading slowdowns and keep systems operating at their best.

Parallelization

One of the most impactful ways to improve performance is parallelization or the technique of breaking large tasks into smaller ones that can run simultaneously across multiple cores or machines.
In distributed computing frameworks, operations on datasets are automatically split into partitions and processed in parallel. Database systems often support parallel query execution, dividing scans and joins across multiple threads. ETL processes can be parallelized by splitting input files, dividing by time windows, or sharding datasets.

For instance, instead of processing a year's worth of clickstream data as one massive job, engineers may break it into daily partitions that are processed in parallel. This reduces job runtime from hours to minutes.

Sharding

Sharding is a specialized form of partitioning commonly used in distributed databases and large-scale data systems. Instead of simply dividing data for faster parallel processing, sharding splits datasets into distinct subsets, called shards, that are distributed across multiple machines or nodes. Each shard is responsible for a portion of the overall data, such as a specific range of customer IDs or geographic regions. This approach allows systems to scale horizontally, handling larger volumes of data and queries than a single machine could manage. Unlike temporary partitions in ETL or batch jobs, shards are persistent divisions of data that ensure both storage and query execution can scale as demand grows [139].

Compression and File Formats

Optimized file formats are another often-overlooked aspect of performance. Columnar storage formats like Parquet and ORC allow queries to read only the columns they need, drastically reducing I/O compared to CSV or JSON. Compression further reduces storage and speeds up queries that rely on scanning large volumes of data.

Observability for Performance

Finally, performance must be measured. Observability tools like query profilers to pipeline metrics dashboards allow data engineers to identify bottlenecks and validate that optimizations are having the intended effect.

Cost Optimization and Budgeting

One of the most common challenges data engineers face is balancing technical performance with financial efficiency. Cloud platforms have made it easy to scale resources up and down, but this flexibility also introduces the risk of runaway costs if workloads aren't carefully managed. Cost optimization in data engineering is the discipline of designing systems that minimize waste, control spending, and align infrastructure use with business priorities.

Cloud Resource Management

The cloud provides virtually unlimited compute and storage, but these resources come at a price since they are billed directly by consumption. Managing these costs is just as important as ensuring performance and scalability. If left unchecked, even small inefficiencies can grow into significant expenses at scale.

Compute usage is one of the largest drivers of cloud costs. Engineers must scale clusters or data warehouses up during heavy workloads and scale them down or suspend them during idle times. Many providers offer built-in features to help with this, such as AWS Auto Scaling or Snowflake's auto-suspend and auto-resume capabilities, which minimize unnecessary compute spend.

Storage management is another critical factor. High-performance storage should be reserved for active, frequently accessed data, while older or less-used data can be shifted into lower-cost storage classes like Amazon S3 Glacier or Google Coldline as we have talked about before. Network costs must also be considered. Data egress fees, especially when moving data between regions or outside of the provider's ecosystem, can add up quickly if they aren't carefully planned for in the architecture.

A key principle across all of these areas is right-sizing, which means ensuring that resources are provisioned no larger than necessary for the workload at hand. By applying this principle consistently, engineers can balance performance, flexibility, and cost efficiency in the cloud.

Query and Pipeline Cost Control

Every query and pipeline carries a cost. Cloud warehouses such as BigQuery and Snowflake often charge based on the amount of data scanned, which means poorly optimized queries that scan entire datasets instead of partitions can multiply expenses quickly. The same principle applies to pipelines. Redundant processes that repeatedly extract or transform the same data consume unnecessary compute resources and inflate cloud bills.

To manage these costs, data engineers can adopt several strategies, some of which we have already touched in performance optimization. Materializing intermediate results helps avoid repeated computation, which is particularly valuable for complex transformations. Regular audits of pipelines can also identify and eliminate processes that are redundant or no longer in use.

In this way, cost optimization ties directly back to performance optimization. Efficient queries and pipelines are faster but also significantly cheaper, creating a win-win for both technical teams and the business.

Budgeting and Forecasting

Cost optimization is also about predicting future costs and preventing surprises. To achieve this, data engineers often collaborate closely with finance and operations teams, ensuring that technical decisions align with business goals.

One important practice is forecasting resource usage based on historical patterns, which provides a baseline for anticipating future demand. Engineers and finance teams can also set budgets and configure alerts within cloud platforms so that teams are notified when spending exceeds expected thresholds. Another key approach is tracking costs at the pipeline or project level, which makes it possible to assign expenses directly to departments and increase accountability across the organization.

Observability for Cost

Just like performance, cost optimization benefits from observability. Monitoring tools such as AWS Cost Explorer, Google Cloud Billing Reports, or third-party tools like Datadog and FinOps platforms, help engineers see exactly where money is going. This allows for quick identification of waste, such as idle clusters, oversized compute nodes, or unnecessary data transfers.

Balancing Cost and Performance

Data engineering is rarely about optimizing for just one factor in isolation. The most efficient query, the fastest storage tier, or the most resilient pipeline will often also be the most expensive. Likewise, aggressively minimizing costs can slow systems down to the point where they no longer serve the business effectively. The real challenge is not to maximize performance or minimize cost, but to strike the right balance between the two.

Prioritizing performance often means investing in premium solutions: high-throughput storage, low-latency networks, and large-scale compute clusters. This approach is necessary for time-sensitive workloads like fraud detection, real-time personalization, or IoT monitoring where delays can mean lost revenue or security risks. The tradeoff is cost. Running these systems at peak performance around the clock can strain budgets, particularly if not every workload requires such speed.

Focusing on cost efficiency typically means leveraging cold storage tiers, spot instances, or batch processing. This works well for workloads such as historical reporting, compliance-driven data retention, or large-scale but non-urgent analyses. However, this savings comes at the expense of performance. Cold storage can take hours to retrieve from, and spot instances may fail or become unavailable. While cost-first strategies are sustainable for background tasks, they may frustrate end users who expect instant results.

Most organizations live somewhere in between. A well-architected system places critical, time-sensitive data in high-performance storage and compute environments, while archiving less-used data in cheaper tiers. Lifecycle policies and hybrid cloud strategies make this balancing act manageable. The art lies in knowing which data needs immediate speed and which can afford delays.

Chapter 13
Data's Invisible Contract

"With great power comes great responsibility."

– Stan Lee [140]

Ethical Data Engineering

Data engineering is often seen as a highly technical discipline, focused on pipelines, storage, and performance. Yet beneath every query and every dataset lies something far more important: people. The data we work with represents human behavior, personal information, and collective trends. With that comes responsibility.

At first glance, ethics may seem like a topic reserved for executives, policymakers, or lawyers, not data engineers. After all, a data engineer's day-to-day work often revolves around building pipelines, writing queries, and managing infrastructure. But the reality is that the systems you design and the choices you make about how data is handled have profound ethical consequences.

Decisions about which data to collect, how to store it, and how to make it available can either reinforce or undermine fairness, transparency, and privacy. For instance, retaining sensitive data longer than necessary could increase the risk of a breach, while poor validation might allow biased or misleading data into downstream models.

Organizations rely on the trust of their customers and stakeholders. A single ethical lapse, such as mishandling private information or exposing user activity through sloppy logging, can damage that trust permanently. Data engineers are often the first line of defense against these risks because they implement the systems that enforce or poorly enforce data protections. Ethical design choices build resilience not just technically, but reputationally.

While regulations like GDPR or CCPA (which we have covered before) provide legal boundaries, laws do not cover every possible scenario. The decision of whether to log sensitive identifiers, replicate data to a less-secure system for convenience, or share datasets across teams often lies with engineers. These choices, whether intentional or not, shape the ethical footprint of a company's data practices.

Balancing Innovation and Responsibility

Data engineers work in environments that push for speed, innovation, and scale. But without an ethical lens, that push can lead to shortcuts with unintended consequences. Building fast pipelines at the cost of ignoring access controls or implementing new tools without considering data privacy might save time now but create far greater risks later. Ethics belong in data engineering precisely because engineers are the ones asked to balance efficiency and responsibility in the daily grind of system building.

Fairness and Bias in Data Systems

One of the most overlooked aspects of data engineering is the role it plays in shaping fairness. While we often think of bias as something that creeps into machine learning models or analytics dashboards, the truth is that bias begins much earlier in the data pipeline. As a data engineer, you are often the one deciding what sources to ingest, how to structure them, and what rules to enforce on their quality. These decisions, even if they appear technical, can have far-reaching ethical implications.

Bias can enter at many stages of the pipeline. If a dataset is incomplete, skewed toward a specific demographic, or collected in ways that exclude certain groups, those blind spots get baked into downstream systems. For example, Amazon famously scrapped an internal AI hiring tool after discovering it penalized résumés that contained words associated with women's colleges or organizations, since it had been trained on past hiring data dominated by men [141].

Similarly, ProPublica's investigation of the COMPAS algorithm revealed that the tool used in the U.S. criminal justice system was more likely to falsely flag Black defendants as higher risk than white defendants, highlighting how historical arrest and conviction patterns reinforced bias in predictive policing [142].

In healthcare, a widely used risk-scoring algorithm was found to underestimate the needs of Black patients because it used healthcare spending as a proxy for illness, and historically underserved groups had less access to care [143]. Even consumer technology has struggled. Facial recognition systems from major tech companies have shown error rates up to 35% for darker-skinned women compared to less than 1% for lighter-skinned men, due to training datasets being dominated by white male faces [144]. Bias can creep in through collection, sampling, and labeling choices, leading to unequal and sometimes harmful outcomes.

Data engineers are uniquely positioned to identify and mitigate bias before it propagates. This might mean questioning whether a data source is representative, checking for systematic gaps in coverage, or pushing back when a dataset appears to underrepresent key groups. Engineers can also build validation checks that surface anomalies in how data is distributed across categories like geography, age, or gender. By embedding these safeguards in pipelines, bias becomes easier to detect early on rather than after a flawed model has been deployed.

Why Fairness Matters Beyond Ethics

Fairness is not just an abstract moral concern. It has direct consequences for business and society. Biased data leads to inaccurate insights, poor decision-making, and in some cases, reputational or legal fallout. The reputational damage and regulatory penalties in such scenarios are often enormous. By keeping fairness in mind, data engineers uphold ethical standards and protect their organizations from costly mistakes.

While engineers cannot solve every problem of bias, they can make meaningful contributions. Techniques like stratified sampling, monitoring distributions over time, and implementing metadata tags that record the origin and limitations of datasets can all help. Transparency about what data can and cannot say is equally important. Sometimes the most ethical act is not to push forward with incomplete or skewed data but to raise the issue and recommend caution.

Privacy and Consent

When working with data, few responsibilities are as important as respecting privacy and obtaining proper consent. Unlike fairness, which is often about ensuring data is representative and unbiased, privacy and consent are about protecting individuals from misuse of their personal information. This responsibility is not optional. Every decision about how data is collected, stored, and shared carries ethical weight and, often, legal implications.

Modern data systems often capture highly sensitive information. Healthcare records, financial transactions, location history, and even behavioral data like browsing habits can reveal intimate details about individuals. If mishandled, this information can be exploited for identity theft, targeted manipulation, or discrimination. Beyond the human cost, breaches of privacy erode trust between organizations and their users. Once trust is lost, it is incredibly difficult to restore, and the damage to reputation and customer relationships can be long-lasting.

Consent is the foundation of ethical data collection. Users should know what data is being collected, why it's being collected, and how it will be used. In practice, this can be messy. Consent forms are often written in confusing legal jargon, or bundled into terms and conditions that most users never read. While you may not write these forms, you are responsible for ensuring that data pipelines respect the boundaries set by user consent. This could mean excluding certain attributes from ingestion, enforcing deletion policies when a user withdraws consent, or flagging datasets that do not meet compliance standards.

Ethical practice goes further. Even in regions where privacy laws are weak or nonexistent, organizations have a responsibility to respect user autonomy. Many global companies voluntarily adopt GDPR-like standards as a baseline, not because they are required to, but because it reflects a commitment to treating user data with fairness and respect. This mindset emphasizes that ethics should not depend solely on what is legally mandated, but on what is right for the people whose data is being handled.

On a technical level, engineers can help enforce privacy and consent by implementing role-based access controls, anonymizing or pseudonymizing data when possible, and maintaining audit trails that show who accessed what information and when. Automating data retention and deletion policies is another key practice, since manually tracking consent-related obligations is rarely feasible at scale. Building these safeguards directly into ETL pipelines and storage systems ensures that privacy is not an afterthought but an integral part of the architecture.

Real-World Examples of Privacy Violations

The importance of privacy and consent becomes clear when we look at high-profile cases where these principles were ignored or mishandled. These incidents demonstrate how quickly trust can be broken and why strong safeguards are not just ethical choices but business necessities.

- Cambridge Analytica and Facebook

  One of the most famous examples is the Facebook-Cambridge Analytica scandal in 2018. A third-party app harvested data from millions of Facebook users, often without their explicit consent, and then used it to build psychological profiles for targeted political advertising. This incident sparked global outrage, damaged Facebook's reputation, and led to billions of dollars in fines and new regulatory scrutiny [145]. Ethically, it highlighted how fragile consent becomes when access is granted through technical loopholes and how indirect data collection can undermine user autonomy if oversight is weak.
- Equifax Breach

  In 2017, Equifax, one of the largest credit reporting agencies in the United States, suffered a breach that exposed the personal data of 147 million people. The compromised records included highly sensitive details such as social security numbers, birth dates, and home addresses. The ethical failure here was in the breach itself and in Equifax's negligence: the company failed to patch known vulnerabilities and delayed notifying the public [146]. The incident underscored how inadequate stewardship of personal data can magnify harm, particularly when organizations hold information that individuals cannot easily change or protect on their own.

Transparency and Accountability

Transparency and accountability form the backbone of ethical data engineering. Transparency means that the way data is collected, processed, and used is visible and understandable to both technical and non-technical stakeholders. Accountability ensures that when mistakes or abuses occur, there's a clear record of who's responsible and what actions can be taken to remediate the situation. Without these two principles, even the most technically secure system can lose the trust of users and regulators.

For a data engineer, transparency often takes the form of clear documentation and auditability. This might include maintaining data lineage maps that show exactly where a dataset originated, what transformations it underwent, and who had access to it along the way. It can also mean exposing metadata, access logs, or processing summaries so that auditors and stakeholders can verify that policies and regulations are being followed. For example, a company that stores personal health records may publish clear usage policies and provide reports showing which teams accessed data and for what purpose.

Accountability goes a step further. Engineers and organizations must be willing to take responsibility when systems fail, when biases are uncovered, or when data is misused. This often requires a culture of blameless post-mortems and rigorous compliance reporting. Accountability mechanisms may also include automated alerts when sensitive data is accessed outside of normal patterns, role-based access controls that tie actions back to individuals, or dashboards that track compliance in real time. These tools make it easier to answer questions like: Who made this change? Why was this dataset shared? Did the use of this data align with stated policies?

When transparency and accountability are absent, public trust can erode quickly. For instance, when organizations fail to disclose breaches in a timely manner or obfuscate how customer data is being used, regulators and customers often respond with backlash. Conversely, companies that make transparency a priority often find it strengthens customer relationships.

Sustainability in Data Engineering

As organizations process ever-growing volumes of data, the environmental consequences of data systems are becoming increasingly difficult to ignore. Large data centers consume massive amounts of water, up to 5 million gallons daily, which is roughly equivalent to the water use of a town with a population of 10,000–50,000 people [147]. The compute resources needed for storage, processing, and machine learning workloads contribute significantly to carbon emissions. Every architectural choice has both a financial and an ecological cost.

An ethical approach to sustainability often means looking beyond performance or cost savings optimizations discussed, and considering the broader impact of engineering practices. Sustainability in data engineering means recognizing that infrastructure choices have ripple effects beyond an organization's bottom line. By embedding ecological awareness into pipeline design and storage practices, engineers contribute efficient systems for a more responsible and sustainable digital ecosystem.

Cloud providers now offer sustainability-focused tools and reporting, such as AWS's Carbon Footprint Tool, Google Cloud's Carbon-Free Energy initiatives, and Azure's Sustainability Calculator. Data engineers can use these tools to help their organizations track environmental impact and directly optimize for greener compute options, such as running workloads in regions powered by renewable energy.

Finally, sustainability ties into the broader culture of responsible data engineering. Just as teams prioritize reliability, security, and compliance, they should also factor in environmental impact when making technical decisions. Choosing efficient algorithms, designing resource-conscious architectures, and consolidating jobs may seem like technical refinements, but collectively they have a measurable impact on energy consumption and emissions.

Chapter 14

A Data Engineer's Bookshelf

"Learning never exhausts the mind."

– Leonardo da Vinci [148]

Resources for the Aspiring Data Engineer

As a data engineer, you must embrace continuous learning and staying up to date with an industry that evolves quickly. Fortunately, there are a wide variety of resources available for those who want to take their skills further, ranging from formal education to free online content.

Formal Education

Formal education remains one of the strongest foundations for entering data engineering. Degrees in computer science, information systems, software engineering, statistics, or related technical fields provide the core skills needed to design and manage data systems. Business analytics and data science programs can also serve as valuable entry points, particularly for those who want to blend technical expertise with applied problem-solving. For working professionals, online programs and master's degrees in areas such as data science or business analytics have become increasingly popular and accessible.

Industry-Recognized Certifications

Industry-recognized certifications are also one of the most effective ways to validate your skills and stand out to employers. A few popular options include:

- AWS Certified Data Analytics – Specialty: Focuses on designing and managing analytics solutions using AWS tools such as Glue, Redshift, and Kinesis.
- Google Cloud Professional Data Engineer: Covers building, maintaining, and securing data processing systems in Google Cloud.
- Microsoft Azure Data Engineer Associate: Concentrates on integrating, transforming, and consolidating data from structured and unstructured sources.
- Snowflake Certifications (SnowPro Core, Advanced Architect, etc.): Specializes in Snowflake's cloud data platform, widely used in modern analytics pipelines.

Alternative Sources

If certifications feel too formal to start, there are plenty of learning platforms offering flexible courses:

- Platforms such as Coursera and edX offer university-backed specializations in data engineering, developed in collaboration with leading institutions such as Harvard University and the Massachusetts Institute of Technology. More broadly, universities around the world have embraced flexible learning models, resulting in a wide range of high-quality, accessible course materials available online.
- Udemy and Pluralsight offer practical, project-driven courses at accessible price points.
- DataCamp focuses specifically on data science and data engineering, with hands-on exercises.
- LinkedIn Learning is an online platform that provides structured courses, tutorials, and learning paths across nearly every discipline. For data engineers, it can be a valuable way to build technical skills, explore new tools, or strengthen related areas like cloud computing, programming, and data visualization.

Self-paced learners have a wealth of free materials at their fingertips:

- YouTube Channels like Data Engineering on YouTube, freeCodeCamp, and individual content creators often break down complex topics into digestible tutorials. I also share content on my own YouTube channel (@Kelvin_Lin_SWE), where I cover topics in data science, data engineering, and software development.
- Articles and blogs that others have written on platforms like Medium and Substack. I regularly write technical articles on Medium (@KelvinLinBU).
- Podcasts and audiobooks on technology and data engineering can be great complements to a morning commute.
- Official Documentation platforms comparable to Apache Spark, Kafka, or Airflow are invaluable for understanding tools

straight from the source.

- Communities such as Reddit's r/dataengineering, Slack groups like Locally Optimistic, or Discord servers provide spaces for Q&A and networking.

There are also excellent books to complement your learning. Titles like *Designing Data-Intensive Applications* by Martin Kleppmann, *The Data Warehouse Toolkit* by Ralph Kimball, or *Streaming Systems* by Tyler Akidau provide depth that goes beyond tutorials. The various white papers mentioned throughout this book are also excellent reads, such as Google's *MapReduce: Simplified Data Processing on Large Clusters* and *In Search of an Understandable Consensus Algorithm* (RAFT) should you want to dive deeper into those topics.

Lastly, nothing replaces hands-on practice. Consider building your own data pipelines with open datasets, contributing to open-source projects (like the many listed in this book), or competing in data engineering challenges on platforms like Kaggle.

Conclusion

The Journey Forward

"Man is still the most extraordinary computer of all."

– John F. Kennedy [149]

What's Next for Data Engineering?

Data engineering is shaped by constant change. As new systems and ideas take hold, the way we handle data shifts with them. Some trends gain traction quickly, others fade, but each introduces new ways to think about scale, speed, governance, and accessibility. For anyone working in the field, keeping an eye on what's emerging is part of staying effective and prepared for what comes next.

Lakehouse Architectures

Traditionally, organizations had to choose between data warehouses and data lakes. Warehouses excelled at structured analytics, offering fast SQL queries and strong governance, but they were expensive and inflexible. Data lakes, on the other hand, could store vast amounts of raw or semi-structured data cheaply, but they lacked the performance and reliability needed for analytics. The lakehouse architecture combines the strengths of both. Platforms like Databricks Delta Lake and Apache Iceberg enable storage of all data types in a single system, while still providing features like ACID transactions, schema enforcement, and high-performance SQL. This means data engineers no longer need to maintain two separate ecosystems and can reduce duplication, cost, and operational complexity. Lakehouses are particularly powerful for organizations that want a unified platform capable of supporting everything from BI dashboards to advanced AI/ML workloads.

Data Mesh

Data mesh is not a single tool or product, but rather a philosophy for managing data at scale. Traditionally, one central data team owns all pipelines and datasets, which often creates bottlenecks as demand for data grows. A data mesh flips this model by distributing responsibility to the domains that generate and use the data. For instance, the product team might own usage telemetry data as a product, while the HR department manages workforce data. Each domain is accountable for ensuring its data is accurate, well-documented, and easy for others to consume. The role of the central data team shifts from building every pipeline to providing shared platforms, standards, and governance so that domains can succeed independently. Although still an emerging concept that requires cultural and organizational change, the promise of data mesh lies in its scalability: decentralizing ownership allows organizations to keep up with growing data needs without overloading a single team.

Automation and AI-Assisted Data Engineering

One of the more recent trends is the rise of AI-assisted tooling within data engineering. Platforms like AWS Glue Studio, dbt Cloud, or even emerging startups are embedding machine learning into their core. These systems can automatically suggest transformations, optimize SQL queries, detect anomalies in pipelines, and even predict bottlenecks. Some tools now feature natural language interfaces, where engineers and analysts can describe transformations in plain English and have the system generate SQL or code automatically. This lowers the barrier to entry and helps teams move faster by reducing repetitive work. While these tools won't replace data engineers, they can augment their work by automating low-level tasks and freeing them up for higher-level problem solving.

Privacy-Enhancing Technologies

With regulations tightening and customers more sensitive about how their data is used, privacy-enhancing technologies (PETs) are becoming a major focus. These include differential privacy, which introduces mathematical noise to protect individuals in datasets, federated learning, which allows models to train across distributed data without moving it, and homomorphic encryption, which makes it possible to compute on encrypted data. This means designing pipelines that do not just move data quickly but also protect it at every step. PETs are still relatively advanced and often costly to implement, but as adoption grows, they will likely become standard features in modern data infrastructure.

The trends I've highlighted here are only a small part of the bigger picture. There are many other approaches and tools that continue to emerge, shaped by business needs, advances in technology, and changes in regulation. By the time you read this, new ideas may already be influencing how data is stored, processed, and governed. Part of being a data engineer is staying curious, paying attention to these changes, and choosing which ones are worth exploring.

Final Notes

Data engineering is a discipline built on both detail and design. At its heart, it's about making data reliable, accessible, and meaningful so that organizations can make informed decisions. The specific tools and technologies will continue to change, but the core responsibilities remain constant: ensuring quality, building scalable systems, protecting sensitive information, and enabling others to work with confidence in their data.

One of the defining aspects of data engineering is that it operates quietly in the background, yet it has an outsized influence on the success of modern organizations. Executives, analysts, data scientists, and product managers all rely on the systems that data engineers put in place. A pipeline that is resilient, efficient, and transparent can accelerate innovation, while a poorly designed one can slow down entire teams or even lead to costly mistakes. The work may not always be visible, but it is foundational.

This book has aimed to provide both the technical foundation and the broader perspective needed to navigate this field. Whether you are designing a simple ETL pipeline or planning the architecture of a large-scale data platform, the same principles apply. Reliability, efficiency, observability, and governance are not optional features but essential qualities of systems that last.

In the end, data engineering is about building a foundation for trust. It's about ensuring that data is not just collected, but prepared, structured, and safeguarded so that it can truly support decision-making. The future will bring new tools and new challenges, but the principles of good data engineering will remain. What matters most is applying those principles with care, so that the systems we build today remain reliable and valuable tomorrow.

The journey of becoming a data engineer never really ends. It is a career defined by continuous learning, by staying curious about emerging technologies, and by always asking how systems can be made just a little bit more reliable, efficient, or transparent. If this book has given you a framework to think critically about those questions and the confidence to start answering them in your own work, then it has served its purpose. The rest is up to you: to keep building, to keep questioning, and to keep engineering the data foundations of the future.

Acknowledgments

Thank you to...

Madison Mercado (@dontmakelies), my unofficial official editor and designer who made this book possible.

And to you, the reader — thank you for picking up my first book and giving these pages your time and attention.

REFERENCES

[1] "Thinking with Computation - Brown Institute." Accessed: Sept. 29, 2025. [Online]. Available: https://brown.columbia.edu/thinking-with-computation/

[2] "Data Scientists," Bureau of Labor Statistics. Accessed: Sept. 26, 2025. [Online]. Available: https://www.bls.gov/ooh/math/data-scientists.htm

[3] "Software Developers, Quality Assurance Analysts, and Testers," Bureau of Labor Statistics. Accessed: Sept. 26, 2025. [Online]. Available: https://www.bls.gov/ooh/computer-and-information-technology/software-developers.htm

[4] "Salary: Data Engineer in United States 2025," Glassdoor. Accessed: Sept. 26, 2025. [Online]. Available: https://www.glassdoor.com/Salaries/data-engineer-salary-SRCH_KO0,13.htm

[5] A. Kay, "Alan Kay | Speaker | TED." Accessed: Sept. 29, 2025. [Online]. Available: https://www.ted.com/speakers/alan_kay

[6] "Wilbour Papyrus," Wikipedia. May 28, 2025. Accessed: Sept. 26, 2025. [Online]. Available: https://en.wikipedia.org/w/index.php?title=Wilbour_Papyrus&oldid=1292637605

[7] "The Babylonians and the Origins of Star Mapping." Accessed: Sept. 26, 2025. [Online]. Available: https://www.mixplaces.com/babylonians-and-star-mapping

[8] "Ancient Greeks Voted to Kick Politicians Out of Athens if Enough People Didn't Like Them." Accessed: Sept. 26, 2025. [Online]. Available: https://www.smithsonianmag.com/history/ancient-athenians-voted-kick-politicians-out-if-enough-people-didnt-them-180976138/?utm_source=chatgpt.com

[9] "z/OS Basic Skills." Accessed: Sept. 26, 2025. [Online]. Available: https://www.ibm.com/docs/en/zos-basic-skills?topic=now-history-ims-beginnings-nasa

[10] "CODASYL Data-Base Management Systems | ACM Computing Surveys." Accessed: Sept. 26, 2025. [Online]. Available: https://dl.acm.org/doi/10.1145/356662.356666

[11] "Edgar F. Codd | IBM." Ac-

cessed: Sept. 26, 2025. [Online]. Available: https://www.ibm.com/history/edgar-codd

[12] E. F. Codd, "A Relational Model of Data for Large Shared Data Banks".

[13] M. M. Astrahan et al., "System R: relational approach to database management," ACM Trans. Database Syst., vol. 1, no. 2, pp. 97–137, June 1976, doi: 10.1145/320455.320457.

[14] D. D. Chamberlin et al., "A History and Evaluation of System R".

[15] "Sequel: A struciured english query language for SIGFIDET 1974 - IBM Research." Accessed: Sept. 26, 2025. [Online]. Available: https://research.ibm.com/publications/sequel-a-struciured-english-query-language

[16] D. D. Chamberlin and R. F. Boyce, "Sequel: A struciured english query language," presented at the ACM SIGMOD Workshop on Data Description, Access and Control, Association for Computing Machinery, May 1974. doi: 10.1145/800296.811515.

[17] W. H. Inmon, "Building the Data Warehouse".

[18] "Data Warehouse Architecture - GeeksforGeeks." Accessed: Sept. 26, 2025. [Online]. Available: https://www.geeksforgeeks.org/dbms/data-warehouse-architecture/

[19] R. Kimball, "Ralph Kimball," Kimball Group. Accessed: Sept. 26, 2025. [Online]. Available: https://www.kimballgroup.com/author/ralph/

[20] "The Data Warehouse Toolkit, 3rd Edition," Kimball Group. Accessed: Sept. 26, 2025. [Online]. Available: https://www.kimballgroup.com/data-warehouse-business-intelligence-resources/books/data-warehouse-dw-toolkit/

[21] "The Data Warehouse Toolkit, 3rd Edition." Accessed: Sept. 26, 2025. [Online]. Available: https://ia801609.us.archive.org/14/items/the-data-warehouse-toolkit-kimball/The%20Data%20Warehouse%20Toolkit%20-%20Kimball.pdf

[22] J. Dean and S. Ghemawat, "MapReduce: simplified data processing on large clusters," Commun. ACM, vol. 51, no. 1, pp. 107–113, Jan. 2008, doi: 10.1145/1327452.1327492.

[23] "Apache Hadoop," Wikipedia. Aug. 26, 2025. Accessed: Sept. 28, 2025. [Online]. Available: https://en.wikipedia.org/w/index.php?title=Apache_Hadoop&oldid=1307839515

[24] "Free Search," Free Search. Accessed: Sept. 26, 2025. [Online]. Available: https://cutting.wordpress.com/

[25] "Hadoop : Components, Functionality, and Challenges in Big Data - GeeksforGeeks." Accessed: Sept. 26, 2025. [Online]. Available: https://www.geeksforgeeks.org/data-engineering/hadoop-components-functionality-and-challenges-in-big-data/

[26] M. Zaharia et al., "Apache Spark: a unified engine for big data processing," Commun. ACM, vol. 59, no. 11, pp. 56–65, Oct. 2016, doi: 10.1145/2934664.

[27] "BigQuery overview | Google Cloud." Accessed: Sept. 26, 2025. [Online]. Available: https://cloud.google.com/bigquery/docs/introduction

[28] "Cloud Data Warehouse - Amazon Redshift - AWS," Amazon Web Services, Inc. Accessed: Sept. 26, 2025. [Online]. Available: https://aws.amazon.com/redshift/

[29] "Kent Beck Quotes (Author of Test-Driven Development)." Accessed: Sept. 29, 2025. [Online]. Available: https://www.goodreads.com/author/quotes/25211.Kent_Beck

[30] "What Is Data Engineering? | IBM." Accessed: Sept. 26, 2025. [Online]. Available: https://www.ibm.com/think/topics/data-engineering

[31] "Without An Opinion, You're Just Another Person With Data." Accessed: Sept. 29, 2025. [Online]. Available: https://www.forbes.com/sites/silberzahnjones/2016/03/15/without-an-opinion-youre-just-another-person-with-data/

[32] K. Lin, "The Extract, Transform, and Load (ETL) Framework with Python," Medium. Accessed: Sept. 26, 2025. [Online]. Available: https://medium.com/@kelvinlinBU/the-extract-transform-and-load-etl-framework-with-python-19d504e1f17b

[33] "Structured vs. Unstructured Data: What's the Difference? | IBM." Accessed: Sept. 26, 2025. [Online]. Available: https://www.ibm.com/think/topics/structured-vs-unstructured-data

[34] "What is Metadata? | IBM." Accessed: Sept. 26, 2025. [Online]. Available: https://www.ibm.com/think/topics/metadata

[35] "Data Drift: How to Detect, Measure, and Handle It | Amplitude." Accessed: Sept. 26, 2025. [Online]. Available: https://amplitude.com/explore/data/data-drift

[36] "ACID Properties in DBMS," GeeksforGeeks. Accessed: Sept. 26, 2025. [Online]. Available: https://www.geeksforgeeks.org/dbms/acid-properties-in-dbms/

[37] "What Is NoSQL? NoSQL Databases Explained | MongoDB." Accessed: Sept. 27, 2025. [Online]. Available: https://www.mongodb.com/resources/basics/databases/nosql-explained

[38] "Data Swamp," Dremio. Accessed: Sept. 27, 2025. [Online]. Available: https://www.dremio.com/wiki/data-swamp/

[39] "Data Marts." Accessed: Sept. 29, 2025. [Online]. Available: https://docs.oracle.com/cd/A81042_01/DOC/server.816/a76994/marts.htm

[40] Redis, "Redis - The Real-time Data Platform," Redis. Accessed: Sept. 27, 2025. [Online]. Available: https://redis.io/

[41] "memcached - a distributed memory object caching system." Accessed: Sept. 27, 2025. [Online]. Available: https://memcached.org/

[42] "A quote from Clean Architecture." Accessed: Sept. 29, 2025. [Online]. Available: https://www.goodreads.com/quotes/9701819-the-only-way-to-go-fast-is-to-go-well

[43] "Shopify API, libraries, and tools," Shopify. Accessed: Sept. 27, 2025. [Online]. Available: https://shopify.dev/docs/api

[44] "Tour of the API." Accessed: Sept. 27, 2025. [Online]. Available: https://docs.stripe.com/payments-api/tour

[45] "JDBC (Java Database Connectivity) - GeeksforGeeks." Accessed: Sept. 27, 2025. [Online]. Available: https://www.geeksforgeeks.org/java/introduction-to-jdbc/

[46] "ODBC Full Form - GeeksforGeeks." Accessed: Sept. 27, 2025. [Online]. Available: https://www.geeksforgeeks.org/dbms/odbc-full-form/

[47] "ODBC Developer's Guide".

[48] "What is change data capture (CDC)? | Databricks on AWS." Accessed: Sept. 27, 2025. [Online]. Available: https://docs.databricks.com/aws/en/dlt/what-is-change-data-capture

[49] J. Kreps, N. Narkhede, and J. Rao, "Kafka: a Distributed Messaging System for Log Processing".

[50] "Confluent | The Data Streaming Platform," Confluent. Accessed: Sept. 27, 2025. [Online]. Available: https://www.confluent.io/

[51] "YouTube Data API | Google for Developers." Accessed: Sept. 27, 2025. [Online]. Available: https://developers.google.com/youtube/v3

[52] "What is Change Data Capture (CDC)? Definition, Best Practices," Qlik. Accessed: Sept. 29, 2025. [Online]. Available: https://www.qlik.com/us/change-data-capture/cdc-change-data-capture

[53] "COPY INTO <table> | Snowflake Documentation." Accessed: Sept. 27, 2025. [Online]. Available: https://docs.snowflake.com/en/sql-reference/sql/copy-into-table

[54] "COPY - Amazon Redshift." Accessed: Sept. 27, 2025. [Online]. Available: https://docs.aws.amazon.com/redshift/latest/dg/r_COPY.html

[55] Infragistics, "Turning Data Into Information," Your Source for UI/UX News and Updates - Infragistics Blogs. Accessed: Sept. 29, 2025. [Online]. Available: https://www.infragistics.com/blogs/turning-data-into-information/

[56] "The Tableau Data Model." Accessed: Sept. 27, 2025. [Online]. Available: https://help.tableau.com/current/pro/desktop/en-us/datasource_datamodel.htm

[57] JulCsc, "Use DirectQuery in Power BI Desktop - Power BI." Accessed: Sept. 27, 2025. [Online]. Available: https://learn.microsoft.com/en-us/power-bi/connect-data/desktop-use-directquery

[58] "cloud.google.com/blog/products/business-intelligence/opening-up-the-looker-semantic-layer." Accessed: Sept. 27, 2025. [Online]. Available: https://cloud.google.com/blog/products/business-intelligence/opening-up-the-looker-semantic-layer

[59] "All Releases - Tableau." Accessed: Sept. 27, 2025. [Online]. Available: https://www.tableau.com/products/all-features#item-102454

[60] "Difference between Star Schema and Snowflake Schema," GeeksforGeeks. Accessed: Sept. 27, 2025. [Online]. Available: https://www.geeksforgeeks.org/dbms/difference-between-star-schema-and-snowflake-schema/

[61] "Dashboards for business users of the Power BI service - Power BI | Microsoft Learn." Accessed: Sept. 27, 2025. [Online]. Avail-

able: https://learn.microsoft.com/en-us/power-bi/consumer/end-user-dashboards

[62] JulCsc, "Use DirectQuery in Power BI Desktop - Power BI." Accessed: Sept. 27, 2025. [Online]. Available: https://learn.microsoft.com/en-us/power-bi/connect-data/desktop-use-directquery

[63] "Data Visualization with Excel and Power BI | Microsoft Power BI." Accessed: Sept. 27, 2025. [Online]. Available: https://www.microsoft.com/en-us/power-platform/products/power-bi/excel-and-power-bi

[64] billmath, "Row-level security (RLS) with Power BI - Microsoft Fabric." Accessed: Sept. 27, 2025. [Online]. Available: https://learn.microsoft.com/en-us/fabric/security/service-admin-row-level-security

[65] "Introduction to LookML | Looker | Google Cloud." Accessed: Sept. 27, 2025. [Online]. Available: https://cloud.google.com/looker/docs/what-is-lookml

[66] "Viewing dashboards | Looker," Google Cloud. Accessed: Sept. 28, 2025. [Online]. Available: https://cloud.google.com/looker/docs/viewing-dashboards

[67] Ugur, "Spreadsheet Sprawl - Uncontrolled Proliferation of Spreadsheets across the Organization: Challenges, Risks, and Solutions.," SpreadsheetWeb. Accessed: Sept. 27, 2025. [Online]. Available: https://spreadsheetweb.com/spreadsheet_sprawl/

[68] "Salesforce Help | Article." Accessed: Sept. 27, 2025. [Online]. Available: https://help.salesforce.com/s/articleView?id=analytics.analytics_overview.htm&type=5

[69] "Learn About Reports and Dashboards | Salesforce Trailhead," Trailhead. Accessed: Sept. 27, 2025. [Online]. Available: https://trailhead.salesforce.com/content/learn/modules/reports-dashboards-quick-look/learn-about-reports-and-dashboards

[70] "API Library | Salesforce Developers." Accessed: Sept. 27, 2025. [Online]. Available: https://developer.salesforce.com/docs/apis

[71] "API Reference Overview," HubSpot docs. Accessed: Sept. 27, 2025. [Online]. Available: https://developers.hubspot.com/docs/api-reference/overview

[72] "Agentic CRM and ERP Solutions | Microsoft Dynamics 365." Accessed: Sept. 27, 2025. [Online]. Available: https://www.microsoft.com/en-us/dynamics-365

[73] "D'Angelo's Wisdom for Realignment in Digital Transformation." Accessed: Sept. 29, 2025. [Online]. Available: https://victoriafide.com/realigning-over-reinventing-applying-dangelos-wisdom-to-digital-transformation/

[74] N. T. Blog, "Netflix Conductor: A microservices orchestrator," Medium. Accessed: Sept. 27, 2025. [Online]. Available: https://netflixtechblog.com/netflix-conductor-a-microservices-orchestrator-2e8d4771bf40

[75] "Airbnb Engineering & Data Science." Accessed: Sept. 27, 2025. [Online]. Available: https://airbnb.io/projects/

[76] "Remarks at the National Defense Executive Reserve Conference | The American Presidency Project." Accessed: Sept. 29, 2025. [Online]. Available: https://www.presidency.ucsb.edu/documents/remarks-the-national-defense-executive-reserve-conference

[77] D. W. W. Rovce, "MANAGING THE DEVELOPMENT OF LARGE SOFTWARE SYSTEMS".

[78] "Home | Scrum Guides." Accessed: Sept. 27, 2025. [Online]. Available: https://scrumguides.org/index.html

[79] "The New New Product Development Game." Accessed: Sept. 27, 2025. [Online]. Available: https://hbr.org/1986/01/the-new-new-product-development-game

[80] Atlassian, "What is a Kanban Board?," Atlassian. Accessed: Sept. 27, 2025. [Online]. Available: https://www.atlassian.com/agile/kanban/boards

[81] K. Beck, "Kent Beck - Software Design Pioneer, Author, Artist & Musician." Accessed: Sept. 27, 2025. [Online]. Available: https://www.kentbeck.com/

[82] "Jira | Issue & Project Tracking Software | Atlassian." Accessed: Sept. 27, 2025. [Online]. Available: https://www.atlassian.com/software/jira

[83] Atlassian, "What is the new navigation in Jira?," Atlassian. Accessed: Oct. 1, 2025. [Online]. Available: https://support.atlassian.com/jira-software-cloud/docs/what-is-the-new-navigation-in-jira/

[84] "Capture, organize, and tackle your to-dos from anywhere | Trello." Accessed: Sept. 27, 2025. [Online]. Available: https://trello.com/

[85] "Create More Social Impact as a Team | Trello." Accessed: Sept. 28, 2025. [Online]. Available: https://trello.com/use-cases/nonprofits

[86] "Manage your team's work, projects, & tasks online • Asana." Accessed: Sept. 27, 2025. [Online]. Available: https://asana.com/

[87] "Master the Asana Interface: A Guide to Key Features and Navigation." Accessed: Sept. 28, 2025. [Online]. Available: https://help.asana.com/s/article/navigating-asana?language=en_US

[88] "Azure DevOps | Microsoft Azure." Accessed: Sept. 27, 2025. [Online]. Available: https://azure.microsoft.com/en-us/products/devops

[89] J. Cool, "Introducing Azure DevOps," Microsoft Azure Blog. Accessed: Sept. 28, 2025. [Online]. Available: https://azure.microsoft.com/en-us/blog/introducing-azure-devops/

[90] "4 ways to use GitLab Issue Boards." Accessed: Oct. 1, 2025. [Online]. Available: https://about.gitlab.com/blog/4-ways-to-use-gitlab-issue-boards

[91] "A quote by Edsger W. Dijkstra." Accessed: Sept. 29, 2025. [Online]. Available: https://www.goodreads.com/quotes/1271018-if-debugging-is-the-process-of-removing-software-bugs-then

[92] "Managing the lifecycle of objects - Amazon Simple Storage Service." Accessed: Sept. 29, 2025. [Online]. Available:

https://docs.aws.amazon.com/AmazonS3/latest/userguide/object-lifecycle-mgmt.html

[93] "Object Lifecycle Management | Cloud Storage," Google Cloud. Accessed: Sept. 29, 2025. [Online]. Available: https://cloud.google.com/storage/docs/lifecycle

[94] "RAID (Redundant Arrays of Independent Disks) - GeeksforGeeks." Accessed: Sept. 27, 2025. [Online]. Available: https://www.geeksforgeeks.org/dbms/raid-redundant-arrays-of-independent-disks/

[95] "How Netflix Uses AWS Compute and Storage Solutions for Global Streaming Innovation - AWS." Accessed: Sept. 27, 2025. [Online]. Available: https://aws.amazon.com/solutions/case-studies/innovators/netflix/

[96] "Home - Chaos Monkey." Accessed: Sept. 27, 2025. [Online]. Available: https://netflix.github.io/chaosmonkey/

[97] "S3 Storage Classes," Amazon Web Services, Inc. Accessed: Sept. 27, 2025. [Online]. Available: https://aws.amazon.com/s3/storage-classes/

[98] "Replicating objects within and across Regions - Amazon Simple Storage Service." Accessed: Sept. 27, 2025. [Online]. Available: https://docs.aws.amazon.com/AmazonS3/latest/userguide/replication.html

[99] "What Is the CAP Theorem? | IBM." Accessed: Sept. 27, 2025. [Online]. Available: https://www.ibm.com/think/topics/cap-theorem

[100] "What is CAP Theorem?," InfluxData. Accessed: Sept. 29, 2025. [Online]. Available: https://www.influxdata.com/glossary/cap-theorem/

[101] "Guarantees | Apache Cassandra Documentation." Accessed: Sept. 27, 2025. [Online]. Available: https://cassandra.apache.org/doc/latest/cassandra/architecture/guarantees.html

[102] "Understand Amazon Aurora high availability and disaster recovery from an Oracle perspective | AWS Database Blog." Accessed: Sept. 27, 2025. [Online]. Available: https://aws.amazon.com/blogs/database/understand-amazon-aurora-high-availability-and-disaster-recovery-from-an-oracle-perspective/

[103] "Relational Database - Amazon Aurora MySQL PostgreSQL - AWS." Accessed: Sept. 27, 2025. [Online]. Available: https://aws.amazon.com/rds/aurora/

[104] "Spanner: TrueTime and external consistency," Google Cloud. Accessed: Sept. 27, 2025. [Online]. Available: https://cloud.google.com/spanner/docs/true-time-external-consistency

[105] "What is Hadoop Distributed File System (HDFS)." Accessed: Sept. 27, 2025. [Online]. Available: https://www.databricks.com/glossary/hadoop-distributed-file-system-hdfs

[106] "PAXOS Consensus Algorithm - GeeksforGeeks." Accessed: Sept. 27, 2025. [Online]. Available: https://www.geeksforgeeks.org/computer-networks/paxos-consensus-algorithm/

[107] D. Ongaro and J. Ousterhout, "In Search of an Understandable Consensus Algorithm".

[108] "etcd." Accessed: Sept. 27, 2025. [Online]. Available: https://etcd.

io/

[109] "Apache ZooKeeper." Accessed: Sept. 27, 2025. [Online]. Available: https://zookeeper.apache.org/

[110] "Manhattan, our real-time, multi-tenant distributed database for Twitter scale." Accessed: Sept. 27, 2025. [Online]. Available: https://blog.x.com/engineering/en_us/a/2014/manhattan-our-real-time-multi-tenant-distributed-database-for-twitter-scale

[111] "PolarDB." Accessed: Sept. 27, 2025. [Online]. Available: https://www.alibabacloud.com/help/en/polardb/

[112] Jamesacowling, "Inside the Magic Pocket." Accessed: Sept. 27, 2025. [Online]. Available: https://dropbox.tech/infrastructure/inside-the-magic-pocket

[113] "logging — Logging facility for Python," Python documentation. Accessed: Sept. 27, 2025. [Online]. Available: https://docs.python.org/3/library/logging.html

[114] "Log Management." Accessed: Sept. 29, 2025. [Online]. Available: https://docs.datadoghq.com/logs/

[115] "The Attack on Colonial Pipeline: What We've Learned & What We've Done Over the Past Two Years | CISA." Accessed: Sept. 27, 2025. [Online]. Available: https://www.cisa.gov/news-events/news/attack-colonial-pipeline-what-weve-learned-what-weve-done-over-past-two-years

[116] "2019 Capital One Cyber Incident | What Happened," Capital One. Accessed: Sept. 27, 2025. [Online]. Available: https://www.capitalone.com/digital/facts2019/

[117] "Summary of the Amazon S3 Service Disruption in the Northern Virginia (US-EAST-1) Region," Amazon Web Services, Inc. Accessed: Sept. 27, 2025. [Online]. Available: https://aws.amazon.com/message/41926/

[118] "Philadelphia District & Marine Design Center > About > Hurricane Sandy." Accessed: Sept. 27, 2025. [Online]. Available: https://www.nap.usace.army.mil/About/Hurricane-Sandy/

[119] "Hurricane Sandy: data center stories from Manhattan - DCD." Accessed: Sept. 27, 2025. [Online]. Available: https://www.datacenterdynamics.com/en/news/hurricane-sandy-data-center-stories-from-manhattan/

[120] "Trust, but verify," Wikipedia. Sept. 11, 2025. Accessed: Sept. 29, 2025. [Online]. Available: https://en.wikipedia.org/w/index.php?title=Trust,_but_verify&oldid=1310777937

[121] "The CPRA." Accessed: Sept. 27, 2025. [Online]. Available: https://thecpra.org/

[122] "Code of Virginia Code - Chapter 53. Consumer Data Protection Act." Accessed: Sept. 27, 2025. [Online]. Available: https://law.lis.virginia.gov/vacodefull/title59.1/chapter53/

[123] "Colorado Privacy Act (CPA)," Colorado Attorney General. Accessed: Sept. 27, 2025. [Online]. Available: https://coag.gov/resources/colorado-privacy-act/

[124] "General Data Protection Regulation (GDPR) – Legal Text." Accessed: Sept. 27, 2025. [Online].

Available: https://gdpr-info.eu/

[125] O. of the P. C. of Canada, "The Personal Information Protection and Electronic Documents Act (PIPEDA)." Accessed: Sept. 27, 2025. [Online]. Available: https://www.priv.gc.ca/en/privacy-topics/privacy-laws-in-canada/the-personal-information-protection-and-electronic-documents-act-pipeda/

[126] "LGPD Brazil - General Personal Data Protection Act." Accessed: Sept. 27, 2025. [Online]. Available: https://lgpd-brazil.info/

[127] "The Privacy Act | OAIC." Accessed: Sept. 27, 2025. [Online]. Available: https://www.oaic.gov.au/privacy/privacy-legislation/the-privacy-act

[128] "PDPC | PDPA Overview." Accessed: Sept. 27, 2025. [Online]. Available: https://www.pdpc.gov.sg/overview-of-pdpa/the-legislation/personal-data-protection-act

[129] O. for C. Rights (OCR), "Health Information Privacy." Accessed: Sept. 27, 2025. [Online]. Available: https://www.hhs.gov/hipaa/index.html

[130] "PCI Security Standards Council - Protect Payment Data with Industry-driven Security Standards, Training, and Programs." Accessed: Sept. 27, 2025. [Online]. Available: https://www.pcisecuritystandards.org/

[131] "Sarbanes-Oxley Act (SOX) | Whistleblower Protection Program." Accessed: Sept. 27, 2025. [Online]. Available: https://www.whistleblowers.gov/statutes/sox_amended

[132] "The Process of Security," Schneier on Security. Accessed: Sept. 29, 2025. [Online]. Available: https://www.schneier.com/essays/archives/2000/04/the_process_of_secur.html

[133] "What is the CIA Triad and Why is it important?," Fortinet. Accessed: Sept. 27, 2025. [Online]. Available: https://www.fortinet.com/resources/cyberglossary/cia-triad

[134] S. Rose, O. Borchert, S. Mitchell, and S. Connelly, "Zero Trust Architecture," National Institute of Standards and Technology, Aug. 2020. doi: 10.6028/NIST.SP.800-207.

[135] "Cybersecurity Framework," NIST, Nov. 2013, Accessed: Sept. 27, 2025. [Online]. Available: https://www.nist.gov/cyberframework

[136] "ISO/IEC 27001:2022," ISO. Accessed: Sept. 27, 2025. [Online]. Available: https://www.iso.org/standard/27001

[137] "The most revealing big data quotes," World Economic Forum. Accessed: Sept. 29, 2025. [Online]. Available: https://www.weforum.org/stories/2015/01/the-most-revealing-big-data-quotes/

[138] "No Silver Bullet," Wikipedia. Nov. 30, 2024. Accessed: Sept. 29, 2025. [Online]. Available: https://en.wikipedia.org/w/index.php?title=No_Silver_Bullet&oldid=1260414372

[139] B. Dipert, "Fully Sharded Data Parallelism (FSDP)," Edge AI and Vision Alliance. Accessed: Sept. 27, 2025. [Online]. Available: https://www.edge-ai-vision.com/2024/05/fully-sharded-data-parallelism-fsdp/

[140] "With great power comes great responsibility," Wikipedia.

Sept. 09, 2025. Accessed: Sept. 29, 2025. [Online]. Available: https://en.wikipedia.org/w/index.php?title=With_great_power_comes_great_responsibility&oldid=1310335076

[141] J. Dastin, "Insight - Amazon scraps secret AI recruiting tool that showed bias against women," Reuters, Oct. 11, 2018. Accessed: Sept. 27, 2025. [Online]. Available: https://www.reuters.com/article/world/insight-amazon-scraps-secret-ai-recruiting-tool-that-showed-bias-against-women-idUSKCN1MK0AG/

[142] J. L. Mattu Julia Angwin,Lauren Kirchner,Surya, "How We Analyzed the COMPAS Recidivism Algorithm," ProPublica. Accessed: Sept. 27, 2025. [Online]. Available: https://www.propublica.org/article/how-we-analyzed-the-compas-recidivism-algorithm

[143] Z. Obermeyer, B. Powers, C. Vogeli, and S. Mullainathan, "Dissecting racial bias in an algorithm used to manage the health of populations," Science, vol. 366, no. 6464, pp. 447–453, Oct. 2019, doi: 10.1126/science.aax2342.

[144] "Study finds gender and skin-type bias in commercial artificial-intelligence systems," MIT News | Massachusetts Institute of Technology. Accessed: Sept. 27, 2025. [Online]. Available: https://news.mit.edu/2018/study-finds-gender-skin-type-bias-artificial-intelligence-systems-0212

[145] "Cambridge Analytica and Facebook: The Scandal and the Fallout So Far - The New York Times." Accessed: Sept. 27, 2025. [Online]. Available: https://www.nytimes.com/2018/04/04/us/politics/cambridge-analytica-scandal-fallout.html

[146] "Equifax Data Breach Settlement | Federal Trade Commission." Accessed: Sept. 27, 2025. [Online]. Available: https://www.ftc.gov/enforcement/refunds/equifax-data-breach-settlement

[147] M. A. B. Siddik, A. Shehabi, and L. Marston, "The environmental footprint of data centers in the United States," Environ. Res. Lett., vol. 16, no. 6, p. 064017, June 2021, doi: 10.1088/1748-9326/abfba1.

[148] "Learning never exhausts the mind...." Accessed: Sept. 29, 2025. [Online]. Available: https://www.oilpaintersofamerica.com/2016/08/learning-never-exhausts-mind/

[149] "Man is still the most extraordinary... John F. Kennedy - Forbes Quotes." Accessed: Sept. 29, 2025. [Online]. Available: https://www.forbes.com/quotes/5248/

www.ingramcontent.com/pod-product-compliance
Lightning Source LLC
LaVergne TN
LVHW022209200926
848481LV00006B/1902

* 9 7 9 8 3 4 8 4 6 4 2 7 1 *